Spotlight Poets

Take a Stand

Edited by Sarah Marshall

Spotlight Poets

First published in Great Britain in 2004 by
SPOTLIGHT POETS
Remus House
Coltsfoot Drive
Peterborough
PE2 9JX
Telephone: 01733 898102
Fax: 01733 313524
Website: www.forwardpress.co.uk

SB ISBN 1 84077 102 X

Foreword

As a nation of poetry writers and lovers, many of us are still surprisingly reluctant to go out and actually buy the books we cherish so much. Often when searching out the work of newer and less known authors it becomes a near impossible mission to track down the sort of books you require. In an effort to break away from the endless clutter of seemingly unrelated poems from authors we know nothing or little about; Spotlight Poets has opened up a doorway to something quite special.

Take a Stand is a collection of poems to be cherished forever; featuring the work of twelve captivating poets each with a selection of their very best work. Placing that alongside their own personal profile gives a complete feel for the way each author works, allowing for a clearer idea of the true feelings and reasoning behind the poems.

The poems and poets have been chosen and presented in a complementary anthology that offers a variety of ideals and ideas, capable of moving the heart, mind and soul of the reader.

Sarah Marshall

Contents

The Authors
& Poems

Bernadette C Curran

I started writing poems in 1995. I now live in Belfast. Since getting married I prefer when writing to keep my poems in my original name of Curran and in the family name.

My poems are a reflection of some of my experiences in life and writing poetry is the best form of personal expression. My work has been recognised and published by various publishers, The International Library of Poetry, The Poetry Guild and Poetry Now. I won the Editor's Choice Award for 1998 for outstanding achievement in poetry by the International Library of Poetry. Also my work appears in a book called *Memories of the Millennium, The Best Poems and Poets of the 20th Century.* Charley Landsborough a great singer and songwriter whom I have met has kept and read some of my poems. It makes me feel very privileged. I love submitting my work to publishers much appreciated. I hope that my poetry in the future will be a source of happiness, comfort and hope, and to reach out to people and give them inspiration.

I would like to say thanks to my husband Jim, to all my family and friends and to the Wave Trauma Centre in Belfast for all their help and support. Especially to my mother Mary, my sisters Margaret, Bridgid, Anna and brothers Peter, Joseph and Liam. Also to my friends, Liz, Rhoda, Charley Landsborough, Philomena, Alana, Rose, Ina, Ann Healey and James and Dympna who are the inspiration in the writing of my poems.

My favourite poets are Seamus Heaney, W B Yates and Ernest Dowson.

To My Friend

When I go to sleep at night I see you in my dreams.
Your smiling face and deep blue eyes that shine before the sun.

Untitled

Every tear of joy that falls each happy
and treasured memory of you is renewed.

In A Dream

In a dream you came to me like an angel in the night
And you were surrounded by a circle of light.
But I need not be afraid of you, our dear sweet child
As I already knew you before you were born.
And if I grieve at your passing,
It's only because I still miss and love you.

A Thought For Today

Sometimes when I have to go away
there's something which I always remember.
That no matter where I am, or whatever path I choose
to walk in through life
there's one path I have already chosen,
that will always lead me back to you.

Evening Glow

(Dedicated in loving memory of Dessie and to all of our loved ones
Who have died in Northern Ireland)

Think of us now we are gone and someday we'll meet again.
Think of us when a new day dawns.
Think of us and know that we shall never be forgotten.
Think of us in your prayers at night.
Think of us when the sun shines bright.
Think of us in this beautiful garden with all the angels and saints,
Surrounded by our loved ones, filled with happiness and peace.
Think of us and all the kindness you showed.
Think of us and all the love you gave.
Think of us and when you feel sad,
Find comfort in knowing that we are always with you.
Think of us for we have walked on and followed in the path
Of God's footsteps which has taken us to Heaven above.

Across The Miles

Under the evening summer sky I walked along the sandy beach
stopping occasionally to look out at the sea.
As distant ships sailed in the deep blue ocean I thought of you
my first true love as I watched the sunset in the golden horizon.
For it's here at this seaside resort I met you many years ago,
we were strangers to begin with, now you're my forever friend.
Although we never married, I guess it was not meant to be,
you filled my days with happiness, and each moment I spent with
you
and the good times we shared will stay with me forever.
For although you are far away across the miles,
I never once forgot you with the passing of time
and even though we are apart, you will always be in my heart
and I know that we will meet again someday.

The Storm

The thunder echoes in the distant hills
and the lightning flashed across the darkened sky.
Standing here alone I look out over the mountains,
as the sheep they run down the heather.
With gale force winds and pouring rain
the wild geese cry out in distress.
While the storm rages on with utter vengeance
leaving behind a path of destruction.
The wild ducks swim away from the lake,
all together stormy weather.

Beyond The Sky

(Dedicated in loving memory of James Lawrence Curran Junior)

Beyond my tears, there's a silent grief
Which is deep within that never goes away.
And as I stood here on the sandy beach looking out at the sea
I whispered a little prayer for you.
The sun it shone in the clear blue sky sending down a ray of light,
As if sent by a divine presence from Heaven above.
For words cannot express the joy,
A new life coming into the world can bring.
But one day our lives changed
When we found out that our child had suddenly passed away.
In our final precious moments with you James,
It seemed as if we had lost a lifetime.
Who knows what the future holds,
But we must never lose hope,
And always remember our treasured memories of you.
Because we know that you are waiting
And watching over us beyond the sky.

Before The Dawn

Today as the sea-blue waves rolled in towards the shore
I thought of you Kathleen.
And as I walked across the golden sand a sense of sadness
Came over me when I found out that you had gone away.
For you were a person in all the years I've known you of unique quality.
Who showed kindness, compassion and love towards me and everyone,
Which at times touched my very soul.
And as I looked up into the late evening turquoise sky
I could see the rainbow.
It seemed to reach out to me like a bridge across the bay.
With its beautiful colours reflecting off the ocean.
As I lay down on the sandy beach I wonder where you are
As the sun sets in the sky.
And with the sound of the ocean, I drifted off to sleep
With my treasured memories and vision of you.
And before the dawn I awake to find you gone.

To Someone Who Cared

(Dedicated to Margaret and for Davey)

To someone who loved me unconditionally
To someone who cared.
To someone who always believed in me while others didn't.
To someone who when I needed a home, a friend,
Or someone to talk to you were there.
To someone who when after James Jnr died,
You knew my sense of loss and pain.
And while everyone else had forgotten him you didn't.
You understood and knew how much we loved him.
To someone who made my life worth living.
To someone I give you my sincere thanks,
And I will always remember and love you
For everything you did for me.
And this is to someone to cared.

A Friend

A friend is someone who cares.
A friend is someone you can trust.
A friend is someone who shows you respect.
A friend is someone who is very special.
A friend is someone you cannot forget.
A friend is someone that you have for life.

Lassie

Where are you now I wonder as I sit here alone.
When the howling of the wind outside
And the slamming of the door broke the endless silence.
I was thinking of my faithful dog called Lassie.
She was an Irish border collie and her coat was black and white.
And for the four years I had her we walked the hills
And crossed the fields together.
One morning I called her and when I went to her kennel she was gone.
Words could not express the sense of loss I felt
That day all those years ago.
The days and nights seem longer now since she went away.
If I ever have another dog maybe in years to come
There's nothing can replace my faithful dog called Lassie.

Until We Meet Again

In the stillness of the late mid summer evening
As I strolled across the white sands,
I was grateful for the moments of tranquillity
I felt from within.
For this beautiful, crystal blue ocean I see before me
Seems to have divided all the years
That we have been apart.
And wherever you are my thoughts are of you,
And through the passage of time
I hope that you will return.
Then we can rekindle the days of our childhood
When we had so much fun.
But I do remember you told me once,
That you always cared for me,
And that you would come back some day.
So as I walked off into the evening sunset,
I cherish those words you spoke to me
Before you went away, that they will come true,
Until we meet again.

Home To Stay

The ocean seemed to meet me as I walked along the sand.
As the waves they crashed against the rocks
I could feel the gentle breeze.
For I was very young when I left my native homeland.
But I always remember the promise that I made,
To come back someday to the place where I was born.
Many years have passed since then, now I have returned.
And cherished are the memories of this country
That I've always known and loved.
With tears of joy and mixed emotions,
I stood for a moment to look out at the sea.
While the sun it shone upon the golden sand,
I feel happy in knowing that this time I'm home to stay.

Missing You

When I thought of you today, my tears they fell like gentle rain,
While across the red evening sky
I could see the beautiful sunset in the horizon.
Standing here surrounded by such beauty and the scenic view,
It seemed to ease the pain of all the years that I've been missing you.
For as the weeks turn into months, my fond memories of you
Keep coming back to me like the ocean waves.
And a time passes by I look forward to the day
When we will meet again.
Until then, I'll wait,
Though I still often wonder why you ever went away.

Allan Bula

I am married, have three children and have seven grandchildren. Have always lived in South East England, first mainly in Croydon, then Guildford, and since 1980 in Bexhill-on-Sea.

Have a degree in economics, but most of my working life has been spent writing publicity material or newspaper reporting or doing other editorial work.

Have long been interested in theosophy; have been secretary of the local United Nations Association for over 20 years; belong to several jazz and light music societies; still go to art classes and try to play the piano; collect books and records as if space and money were infinite; and am a life member of the Swedenborg Society.

Am an adviser on Dr Matthias Rath's Cellular Medicine formulas, which are based on the premise that the health or disease of our bodies is decided at the level of millions of body cells. Following the death of my elder daughter at the age of 40, due to breast cancer spread to the brain, I've become even more interested in health defence, and welcomed Dr Paul Clayton's book of that name, as well as Dr Rath's publications.

First literary influences were Grimms' fairy stories read at home and the poems of Keats, Shelley and Wordsworth read at school. Yet my own light verse seems more reminiscent of Ogden Nash! As a compulsive writer, I don't only scribble poetry, but also a lot of letters to others and diary and notebook entries to myself.

The literary influences of my youth were the essayists William Hazlitt and Ralph Waldo Emerson. Indeed, Emerson rescued me from much teenage anxiety!

The Magic Elsewhere

Oh, my first day at school was traumatic,
For I was a stay-at-home fanatic
And being forced to stare at a blackboard
Made me feel just restless and not adored.

And where was my friend next door that first day?
If I'd seen him I'd have agreed to stay.
Could our parting have been some adult plot
To soften us at once to our new lot?

Then, miracle! I went back after lunch.
Perhaps even then I had had a hunch
That, despite my deep shock, school was a place
Around which there were better things to face.

On the corner was Bellinger's, a shop,
Which soon became my most regular stop,
I found sherbet dabs and aniseed balls
And could not resist their sweet, siren calls.

Thus, at five, I learned how to be content,
Even when not liking the main event.
Do not shirk, always do the thing you must,
But in the magic elsewhere put your trust.

Reading Calls

All my life, I've loved pianos galore.
If I could play, I'd love them even more.
But, as a beginner, I stayed quite still,
Advancing not at all in keyboard skill.
Then drawing and painting attracted me
But I couldn't show what my eyes could see.
I tried a representational act,
Yet got a picture looking quite abstract.
As a result, my books came to the fore -
In fact, at times, they almost blocked the door.
That 'my books' wasn't said as a writer,
A role that would be markedly brighter.
No, my part is unbridled collector,
Which of space is just not a respecter.
In most of my rooms, books line all the walls.
Eyes may tire, but the lure of reading calls.

Five Minutes Yet

Upon a cold December 28th,
I drove for sixty icy miles to church.
In this fine building was my friend to wed,
But first I needed nature's call to heed.
Alas, no haven was there anywhere,
But soon appeared a man with aged stride.
'Oh Sir,' I called with firm but plaintive voice,
'Where is the nearest public toilet place?'
'About a mile,' he said in bleak reply.
My look of total resignation must
Have stirred his heart to action very well,
So prompt was invitation to his home.
A fifteen-minute walk as all it took
To make me calm and wedding-fit again.
But now the call of nature pressed my wife,
Who waited car-borne - patient, growing tense.
'Fear not,' I soothed, 'we've still five minutes yet.'

Just Thin Out The Right Angles!

New York once had a skyline
That was thought to be quite fine.
In fact, plans were soon unfurled
For copies throughout the world.
Now it seems straight up and down
No longer makes a fine town.
Ninety degrees won't make it.
To get a winning ticket
And to overcome wrangles,
Just thin out the right angles!
Jagged slopes will give delight
On the nine-eleven site.
Berlin, Salford and Bilbao
First followed this switchback tao,
Pioneering oblique style,
Now set for a New York trial.
My view is from well below -
I'd prefer a bungalow.

A Cool, Low-Stress Affair

True love is something way beyond control,
Because it's not foreseen by any soul.
Indeed, it bursts ungreeted in, without
First checking that it has been thought about.

To such a storm, you can't acclimatise,
Because it comes as such a huge surprise.
Demanding, like a blinding twist of fate,
Love's hard for most folk to accommodate.

It shows our normal days in eerie light
And, circling us, quite soon benumbs all fight.
But less dramatic states are more relaxed
And leave your hard-worked heart much, much less taxed.

For, shorn of transports of delight, our life
Is also, thank the Lord, less prone to strife.
The goal to which this verse most wisely tends?
A cool, low-stress affair between just friends.

I Love A Piano

At eleven, keyboard lessons were my desire,
Radio pianists having set my dreams on fire.
I aimed to do a passable imitation
Until I faced practice and all its frustration.
Two teachers, one young and one old, fell to my lot,
But both were at one in thinking me not so hot.
Teenaged Olive Coleman scorned my musical choice,
But old Flora Dixon was moderate of voice.
Her mature help guided me through many a test,
Although her taste in pieces did reduce my zest.
Also, my home piano was old, stiff and slow,
Which made for performances which just didn't flow.
So, despite knowing it was the excuse of fools,
Like a poor workman, I started blaming my tools.
Yet, if my prowess could be put in a thimble,
At least all the effort kept my fingers nimble.
Now, when I can play only half as well as then,
My hands are still as supple as they were at ten.

Less Dress, Toil And Fattening Food

June, July and August are great
But too much heat can be their fate.
Then clothing is cut to the bone
(Or rather skin) and left alone.
Sunglasses and shades both come out
But much else we must do without.
Yet our garden of a few sticks
Now needs more than one or two ticks.
This is awkward, for what does irk
In heat is any kind of work.
So on these joys of summer brood -
Less dress, toil and fattening food.

Auntie's Lifelong Lunar Link

The night my aunt was born, the moon was full.
We know, because we've checked the phases chart.
Of course, this proof did not come overnight.
Indeed, it wasn't known until the day,
When Uncle's curiosity was roused.
At school and, later, pension-time, he found,
Aunt's deeds had flowed in lunar cycles all.
When young, to Brighton walked she, moonlight-lit -
A fair old step from London trod by night.
A Max (the cheeky chap) Miller fan,
She only laughed at him on lunar nights.
Her housework too was governed so, besides
Home-sitting, also slave to Aunt's decree.
And moving flat by day, she showed the same
Persistence - Auntie's lifelong lunar link.
So mums-to-be, hold back or push - ensure
The night your babes are born, the moon has waned.

His Short Foray As Mr Chips

Unlicensed was the teacher, who bereft
Of training, true vocation, not to say
Aplomb and vital bits of paper, tried
To stand before a class with pride and teach.

Geography and English were his claims
To competence and temporary sway.
Brazil and Zealand, New, he offered, nay
Imposed on geographic pupils all.

At breaktime, playground duty had to be
A turn our hero took. To end it, he
Employed a whistle far beyond compare -
A red and yellow Christmas cracker gift.

This plastic toy endeared the temp to more
Discerning boys, who gathered round him, full
Of cries of, 'How are you Sir?' loud enough
To wake the street, long after he'd resigned.

In age, eleven, twelve and thirteen were
His forms - attentive if advanced, but not
If less adept. In fact, the backward group
Behaved to justify its name for shame.

How stark the contrast 'tween his best class and
The worst! Receptive were the cream and quite
Defiant were the duds. But both as stars
Lit up his short foray as Mr Chips.

Bring Back Pictures In The Fire

Living room fires used to dictate which way to face.
Now hordes of televisions have taken their place,
Shaping how we arrange the chairs
While distracting us from our cares.
On today's mantelpiece, above the screen
As usual, plants and greeting cards are seen.
And the box resembles an old friend
Who, should we at times to slumber tend,
Like an indulgent pal, doesn't mind,
Sleep being not all it helps us find.
We saw pictures in the fire in days of old,
A plus freely added to relief from cold.
So are scenes contrived with skill and sent to lure
Less boring? Frankly, viewers aren't always sure.

Optimist In Residence

Optimist in residence was Robert
Muller's unofficial title, earned through
Thirty-eight years' UN service, keenly
Given in the most campaigning spirit.

Testament to the United Nations,
Robert's farewell book, proclaimed his passion,
Positive approach and love of peace for
All, through constant international effort.

'Organise and institutionalise we
Must as humans,' said he. But the challenge
Was to do it wisely, aiming high for
Love, co-operation, good and welfare.

Chancellor, University for Peace, in
Sunny Costa Rica, was this preacher's
Next position. Prophet-like, he drafted
Ten commandments, urging outlooks global.

Next came ten for groups and institutions.
These he linked to personal creed and promise.
Three supreme commandments crowned his gospel:
You shall love the Earth and God and others.

We are used for something special on our
Unique planet. If we understand that
We'll succeed. But if we don't, the cosmos
Something else will try. The choice is ours now.

This was Robert's oft-repeated message,
Dreaming this millennium would be the
First ten hundred years of peace. Such was his
UN wish for our today and future.

Sympathy For Life

My first job was delivering the Christmas post,
An exploit about which I've never ceased to boast.
Three times a day, the last by the light of a torch,
For ten days we were in first this, then that strange porch.
Denis Holloway did the right side of the street,
I the left, that first time we realised we'd got feet.
When no one was in, I left mail with next-door folk,
Only to be warned once - *those* neighbours never spoke!
Wet, dry, rain, sun, ice, snow - varied weather was rife,
Ensuring all postmen my sympathy for life.

The Samaritan Had The Essence

Once paganism held all the world under its spell,
Now Christianity is an ancient faith as well.
Crucified and born again are the great issues stressed,
When on new prospects the fervent Christian views are pressed.
Resurrection is the big point, but most of us find
It hardly matters compared to the need to be kind.
Centuries of theological effervescence,
Yet the Samaritan already had the essence.
Resurrection or not, it's the golden rule which could,
If practised by all, bring paradise to Earth for good.

Most Felt, Least Understood

Love, a most felt but least understood feeling,
Craves care in all degrees with which we're dealing.
An example is an ex-girlfriend's mother
Although it could quite well be someone other.
Long after her dear daughter to me had cooled,
One mother protested at being so ruled.
'You never come to see us now,' she complained,
A truth which was easier said than explained.
Alone together at a theatre just once,
With this older partner I'd felt a mute dunce.
Never having been a teenager before,
I didn't know such a state was natural law.
We had gone to see The Winslow Boy, a play
Which showed youth must be seen to choose the right way.
Morally uplifted but confused inside,
I decided the friendship should be denied.
But with better control of feelings and fact,
That warm link should have been saved with care and tact.

Who Knows What Wonders . . . !

To do anything for a rhyme -
Is that such a terrible crime?
Pop fans now think rap is magic,
While outsiders call it tragic.
Once some poets used to await the muse,
Yet others artificial aids would use.
Verse may be read to escape TV,
Although writing it too this ruse can be.
How often has telly been the reason
To switch to something else for a season?
Thus the box may swell evening classes
And, at pubs, fill many cheering glasses.
Not only viewing figures should be read
But word of what non-viewers do instead.
The little screen, an occupying force,
Makes thoughtful non-conformists change their course.
So who knows what wonders are being done
By those who don't think watching all is fun!

Untroubled Mind

At night, review wise thoughts of yesteryear.
The woe that seems so new to you is old.
In other places, other times, the strain
Of trouble made the thoughtful pen response.

For instance, 'work the best narcotic is',
And 'don't despair, but if you do, work on';
Plus 'act for good and hope for good and take
What comes' - all formulas for fortitude!

'This day,' Columbus wrote determinedly,
'We sailed on,' adding just, 'course west, south west.'
What difficulties did this brief note hide?
'We cry inside,' a recent version says.

Such lines-to-live-by force our hopes to rise.
'Make me an instrument of peace,' we cry,
And reap the calm from heartfelt focus change,
Recovering thought and feeling lost just now.

All wisdom to the same conclusion comes.
For one thing only, any price is worth.
'On my head, pour a sweet serenity.
Untroubled mind, please give me now,' we pray.

Denise Everitt

My name is Denise Everitt. I live in a small town called Castleford near Wakefield, I am 39 years old, I have three grown up children, two boys and one girl. Two of my children live at home with me, my oldest son has now a family of his own and made me a nana so I have a little grandaughter called Chloe who is one year old.

I look after my father most of the day and my children. When I have time I like drawing and reading books. I started writing poems last year when I started going to Castleford Spiritualist Church which I am now attending lessons to improve my mediumship. I have always been aware of spirits since I was a young child and used to talk to an old man no one else could see. I can sense, see and hear them and have given lots of evidence for people in church.

I hope my poems can inspire people, and let them know when their loved ones die it's just the body which dies, the spirit lives on.

A Mother's Bond

(This was written for someone who was
not talking to his mum when she died)

A mother's bond never breaks,
For we all make mistakes.
So it is now we make amends,
For our friendship never ends.
On a night when we all sleep
I sometimes used to hear you weep,
But that was oh so long ago and there's one thing
That you must know,
In this life we did not speak,
And with that I fell asleep.
But no more sorrow, no more pain,
For I loved you all the same.
I never stopped, I never would,
For you were sent from Heaven above.
So with this poem I send my love,
And say goodnight and God bless, love.

Dad

At the back of the room in his home,
Our father sits alone,
Alone there by the phone,
Hoping to hear the tone.
Ring, ring, ring,
My eyes do sting,
To watch him there gasping for air,
Wondering if his daughters care.
Yet he would be fit
If he did not have to work down the pit,
So please pick up the phone,
You too may end up alone.

We Each A Number

Oh mirrored soul thy secret holds,
Within our heart life's pathways start
Not one path holds the spirit's goal.
Many walks the path unfolds,
Nearer perfection of God's selection,
Hence do we die, or do we lie
In sleeping slumber we each a number.
Throughout our life,
We sometimes wonder.
What day, what time,
He will call our number,
Then back again in sleeping slumber.

The Lord's House

Close your eyes, go to sleep,
Hush, be quiet, please don't weep,
For in my house there is no pain,
And in my house there is no shame,
For to me you are all the same.
A king, a queen it does not matter
A tramp, a beggar or whatever.
Within my house you will have no fame,
Within my house there is no gain.
So learn to love your fellow men,
For you're all equal in the end.

Missing You

(Wrote for Mum with love)

I went to sleep and you were there,
My loving mother so tender, fair.
Eyes like emeralds which shone so bright
All around you, a golden light.
You tried so hard to stay and fight,
But you were gone come early light.
A soul so tender, your heart surrendered,
Into God's arms and Heaven's charm,
Free from pain, you now remain
In God's care where you can share
Your love for children, and adults too.
No one will ever walk in your shoes
And even though I was only eight,
God had already made that date
And he did not want you to be late.
Everyone missed you, when you went,
But God did not give us you,
He just lent you, to us for a while,
Because he too wanted to see your smile.

What Is Love?

Love is the first time you look up into your mother's eyes.
Love is the first time you hear your baby's cry.
Love is a father who works all his life.
Love is a man who stands by your side.
Love is compassion and goodness within.
Love is to reach out to someone in need.
Love it begins with a small, tiny seed.
Love is to unlock your heart, to be free.
Love is to always put others first.
Love is to not forget your own self worth
Because if you don't respect yourself,
Your self-esteem stays on the shelf,
Never knowing nothing else,
The real you shines within,
So pure and bright, don't let it dim,
A being of light so get it right,
A seed of love from Heaven above.

Childhood Memories

I had a doll which was so sweet
She used to sit upon my knee,
A baby doll with all her charm
I used to carry in my arms.
But then I grew up like the rest
And forgot my doll who was the best,
She never cried, she never moaned
She never said, 'Oh Mum come home.'
You're never in, you're always out,
And with this we always shout
But they must know when they were young,
I never left them for so long,
It's only now that they have grown
I spend a little time on my own.

The Buffalo

The Indian stands upon the hill,
Looks for the buffalo to make his kill,
The buffalo grazes and stands alone,
Leaves his herd and off he roams,
Deeper into the country he goes
But the Indian's fast on his toes,
Fast as lightning the brave attacks.
Runs the buffalo with a dash,
Darting and dashing to make his escape,
But for buffalo it was too late,
The Indian's spear was fast and straight,
And so the buffalo's life was erased.

Silent Whisper

I shout your name but you don't hear,
I stroke your face. Look I am here.
But you don't know, you think I have gone,
I cry out, 'No my spirit lives on!'
No more pain, no more sorrow,
For there is no more sad tomorrow,
For I laid down my earthly coat,
And floated away with my heavenly host,
But my friend we will meet again,
So for now let us pretend,
That I have gone just for a while,
And one day you'll be by my side,
For our love will never die.

Jordan

*(I wrote this poem for a neighbour's little boy
who passed away aged 1½)*

Just over the moon not far away,
On a night is where I play,
Run and skip then I sip fizzy orangeade,
Down again it never ends, for I am a special child,
An angel sweet, I fell asleep and all my love I send,
Never fear for I am still near and never far away.

Rivers Run Home

I sit on the bank and give out a sigh,
I look to the side, the river is high,
So dark and mysterious so deep, so tranquil
One of life's mysteries as old as the hills
I throw a stick to see what it does
Sends ripples along it and in falls some mud
Some parts are foggy, some parts are clear
But they keep on going and flowing with ease
Each river is different, its own speed it goes
Some may be lucky which have a straight road
Others have bends and dead ends they meet
But they keep on running without any feet
A force which keeps pulling an energy strong
For it's Mother Nature the rivers flow on
So they're on a journey just like you and me
And their journey ends when they meet the sea
Some may be faster, some may be slow
But it does not matter for they all reach home
The journey of life is what's it's about most,
People live in God's loving light,
Others they stray and bad deeds they do
Paths of oblivion is the life that they choose.

Shadows Of War

A ray of hope on darkened land,
Grains of silver shine in the sand
United allies hand in hand,
Friend or foe, yet many woes,
Of tortured souls and war heroes,
Humans restricted by dictatorship,
Words of domain upon his lips,
Hence his country dark in eclipse,
Under the rule of his leadership,
In fear and gloom shadows loom,
Under conflict and rubble there lays his tomb,
So now resume your land of free,
Happy times, no misery.
Then remember the men from the west,
Who came to help and did their best,
Hence freed you from your bondage chains,
Who lost their lives in freedom's name.

Peace In The East

A blush of red high in the sky.
Roars of planes through eastern sky.
Sounds of children's weeps and cries
Soldiers walk on native land;
Under foot there is but sand,
No grass's green, just horrors seen,
Brought upon humanity.
Hence when will it redeem?
Apparently not yet it seems
For peace is made in dreams.

Memories

I looked through the mirror,
A stranger looked back.
Most of my life it has been rather black,
Family and friends I have lost on the way.
Oh how I prayed and wished they could stay,
But it could not be and now they are free,
No more pain for them or me,
The hurt inside as I said my farewell,
To watch them suffer was my own living hell,
But now they're at peace and at rest,
Memories and love stay close to my chest,
Their life and love stay locked in my heart,
For every minute we are apart.

Mother's Love

A mother's love never dies.
For she waits up in the sky
And one day you will meet again,
A kindred spirit never ends.
Smell her smell, feel her touch
Because she loves you very much.
So on a night when we sleep,
You may feel a hand upon your cheek,
Don't be sad, please don't cry,
It's only Mum to say goodnight.

The Old Man

A summer's morning you can see,
the sun is dawning beyond the trees
overlooking a calm blue sea.
An old man walking on the sands
takes a look at his tired old hands,
his fingers crooked, his bones ache too,
his sight is dim but he just gives a weary grin,
for he knows his time is near,
then he can rest his weary head,
and join his friends who are all dead.
As waves crash upon the shore,
he takes a look, just once more,
for he knows his time is here
home he goes and disappears,
to rest his head upon his bed.
Come the morning, he is dead.

For A Moment

*(This was wrote for my niece's little baby
Leoni who only lived for a few hours)*

Before I was born my work was done,
Because I was a chosen one.
A special child full of grace,
I never walked upon this place,
But I was lucky can't you see,
For I saw you and you saw me,
So with my love, I send a flower,
To grow and bloom in the April showers,
Her name's Leoni and she smells sweet
To let you know that we just sleep,
And when you look up to the stars,
You'll know that I am never far.

My Life

In my life there is no control,
Even when I play my role
A mother, a daughter, a sister too.
But most of all a friend for you,
A simple thank you is all I ask,
Yet nobody seems to get my grasp,
They talk to me like I am dirt,
Never realising how much it hurts,
My husband ran away with a friend,
And when they did that we still made amends.
Names I have been called throughout my life,
Emotional trauma and lots of strife,
Helping people that's all I did wrong,
And now the time's come for me to be strong,
To walk the path which I belong,
A path of courage is what it is,
For I have already learn to live,
To lose my mum when I was eight,
And when I was young to lose a mate,
But I will never forget those dates
For I can say sorry, for some it's too late.
So it is now I make a stand, as I walk upon this cruel land,
Instead of putting others first, the time has come to put me first,
A little respect is all I ask, so I can remove my unhappy mask,
And still carry on to do all the tasks,
Instead of stopping a chore that I do, so I can come running
To look after you, please think of me the next time you moan,
Because in the end I too have a home.

Victor Shaw

Hi. My name is Victor Shaw. I currently live in Northern Ireland. Or if you prefer the North of Ireland. I am originally from Birkenhead, but grew up in Northern Ireland. Thus the reason why I class myself as Irish, and with some reluctance, I am also, very British. My family, is very important to me. They consist of two loving grans, a devoted mum and dad, two special sisters, one blessed brother, three nieces who are real princesses, and one gem of a nephew. My aunts, uncles and cousins also play a big part in my life, and I am always adding a new poem to my vast collection, when there be a new addition to the family, which, I hold so dear!

I often wonder to myself, why do I write poetry? The main reason, would be thus! To give other people enjoyment. I get a kick, from other people's emotions. And if, only one person likes just one of my poems, then I have achieved my aim. Simple pleasures, for simple minds, that's what I say. I am contented, just! At the very least just at being read. Everything else, is an added bonus!

To the question, what inspired me to write and what be my influences? The answer would indeed be thus! I started off, with a very low standard of education, and for a large amount of early childhood, I was in special needs classes. This in turn, gave me a thirst for knowledge, and a deep desire to better oneself. To begin with, my poetry was very simplistic, but it did get better after thirteen years of hard work. And finally I started to see the benefits of my work, with the publishing of some of my poems by Forward Press, whom I will be always indebted to.

PS I would like to say, that this book wouldn't have been possible, without the help of *Maureen Kirkpatrick*, for whom, this book is especially for. *With love.*

Meaning

Every man needs his mother,
The same as
Every sister needs her brother.
Every little kiss has a meaning,
The same as
Every slight touch has deeper feeling,
Every thought can be a passing pleasure,
The same as
Every memory an uncountable treasure.
Every loving care can be lost,
The same as
Every regret can have its cost.
Yet happiness is only found in the feeling,
For everything in life
Knows only love and meaning?

True Love

Love without another secret desire!
Wild passion within the sensual fire!
To have kindness
Without the blindness!
To have and to hold
With sheer need,
Without the written deed!
Such would be the chemistry!
Without the embittered jealousy!
Always enjoying the long embrace,
As you trace
The detailed lines on that
Special face!
To love with an open heart!
Is love, from the complete start!

A Rare Face Of beauty

I saw a well-cultivated English garden,
Around, a refined golden field.
White columns, stretched forever onwards,
As wild poppies, attracted,
Blowing before they yield.
Next? A hollow hive,
Where, sweet fragrance would often fly.
Beyond that?
Two pools collected,
Heaven's wishes,
Dropping from on high.
I viewed, two blackthorn hedges,
Then? A well-worn track!
Clear visions, gathered in the harvest,
While, the field? Was turned, so black?

The meaning of this poem!

Line one. A woman's mind.
Line two. Her golden skin.
Line three. Her white teeth.
Line four. Her red lips.
Line five. Her nose.
Line six. Her eyes.
Line seven. Her eyebrows.
Line eight. Her furrows.
Line nine. That's seeing such beauty!
Line ten. As the memory, ending!

Dream Of Dreams

Her hair was as golden like fresh summer's hay!
How beautiful those sharp pearls of blue,
Revealed, only with joy's sweet play!
Wonderful in spirit! As wild as it was free!
And how I wish! She would, never let me be!
The mind so innocent!
As that heart so pure!
And what pains for her!
Would I gladly endure!
My love! Is for her stark beauty!
As well as her ways!
Which, all mortal men could only love!
Or all of their days!
A faint smile, from those rose-blessed lips,
Would melt the hardest of hearts!
And everything she does to me
Becomes as priceless,
As jewelled arts!
Her graven pity!
Would release a guilty man!
While making the hangman cry!
And as for her love?
It's where the highest treasure, does lie!
Yet she has many a fair prince,
To choose from!
To do her lawful bidding!
She appears to have only eyes for me!
And with all of my sinning
For this reason
Only her heart will ever know
Thus! The reasons why!
I love her so.

Wisdom For Children

If grappling with the mind's eye,
And still you fail, no matter what you try.
Never struggle onward with bated breath,
Or there will be an untimely death.
Act like a spider with nothing to do,
Then liken to a fly, it will come to you!

Cold War

While silence is waiting, to be broken!
Words are not best left unspoken!
The mind will work temperance to the bone.
As feelings are always waiting, to be shown!
Bridges may be waiting, to be crossed
But chance will always weigh up
This heavy cost!
This real wonder has to be seen
For only true love
Can ever make us
So mean!

Fairest Of The Fair

So full of grace and air,
I beg to stare!
For she holds, such pride of place!
Among many a sweetest rose
Deemed so pure,
Yet even more so rare!
She can care for dear nothing!
No idle word can I muster, or dare!
She will I am sure go to another?
I'll swear! And again I'll swear!
Till, I am, old and grey,
I'll ever forget,
Such, a shining face!
Filled with absolute joy!
Whilst my heart, be in abject despair!
For she alone be the brightest,
Of the bright!
And the fairest
Of the fair!

A Pilgrim's Progress

You are my sun, moon and air!
My ray of hope, in darkest despair!
Your light shines the appointed way,
If only, I could make you stay!
Then homewards would my journey be,
As my heart and spirit belongs to thee!

Peacetime

A time of new hope,
And of a new dawn!
With another turn of the corner
All our troubles could be soon, gone!
Mothers will now sing, to their children
A new, unfamiliar song!
For a time of real bitterness
Has been, and now gone!
Let children with unworried eyes, sleep!
As again, sweetness in laughter,
Is once more heard on the street!
While brothers and sisters
Unite! Hand upon hand
For no more blood will be spilt
On this truly majestic land!
Let praise be
For sending thy dove!
The most precious gift
Given from dear Heaven above!
It is then
Sweet smiles, can be born, and then released!
For it is only then
We all can find the true wonder
Of love! Joy and peace!

Going To Work

Steady as a heartbeat,
with shadow racing on.
Moving with conviction,
mouth open for a yawn.

Routine makes reluctance,
while time adds the dread.
These things give us substance,
whilst getting out of bed!

The Graveyard

Here stands the mere monuments,
Dedicated to lost breath!
Standing out like pointed fingers
As if to remind us
We all must in turn
Greet and meet our death!
We offer, a token, flower,
To a past and distant memory!
Telling their spirit
We miss them so!
Asking deep within our hearts
Will we meet again?
We the living,
Can never know!
Stone guardians, watch forever weeping,
At the remembrance,
Of all those long spent tears!
Leading all the souls upwards,
Having wasted most of their earthly years!
All had so little time!
Yet so much
To give!
And through us the mere living
They shall always continue, to love
Forever good start
Must, alas have its bitter end!
Yet, every stone here
Is forever carved,
In the hearts and memory,
Of time,
Lover
And friend.

Summer

Illumination sought me!
As Pan played a melodic tune!
Nor treasures did I see, till then!
For only light
Revealed the boon!
We all gathered up the glory!
Like taking up, our share!
Given to such wonder!
We lived life
Without a care!

Only You

May God grant us, a truly beautiful day,
With the heavenly sun and moon are in their state and play!
May the stars dance, away above your sweet, golden head?
As in all things, our mutual strong love is now, read.
I picture it among the great seas of this majestic earth,
As they murmur their satisfaction,
For even they will come to know! For your divine pureness in worth!
I hope and long for your deep sensitive touch,
For it alone blesses many a sandy shore.
For I wish to be with you, hopeful? Of for evermore
All until, I'll be finally lost! For mere moral words.
As you bring charm and grace, to even the smallest in birds!
While your light touch, opens the very heads, of beautiful flowers,
Yes, I could sit and listen to you,
In awe, especially in all them lonesome hours!
What I'm I to do? For I have become so totally captivated,
Liken to a great bad cat, I am mindful, and completely fascinated.
Such wit! As there is such delicate grace,
As I watch time now spent,
Through the eternal blessings
Now falling on your angelic face!
You are as warm, like a radiant sunshine!
And I am so glad
That you are always going to be mine!
For, I don't know
What I would do
If I wasn't loving
Only you!

Antrim

Travelling in a thousand places
But, in my heart
You still strike, a chime
In every street
Old familiar faces
As if enchantment
Takes part, of time!

Nature, never fixed, a golden vision,
More enticing
While moving,
In a curvaceous, lush way!
Sprinkling my childhood cake
With snow-capped icing
As pure silver, in wishes
Is given
To Lough Neagh!

Questions Of A Living Soul

Where are the living without the dying?
Where is the laughter without the crying?
Where are the sane without the madness?
Where is the happiness without the sadness?
Where is the war without the peace?
Where is the famine without the feast?
Where is the fool without the wise?
Where is the truth without the lies?
Where is the day without the night?
Where is the blind without those with sight?
Where is the weak without the strong?
Where is the right without the wrong?
Where is the damned without the saved?
Where is the coward without the brave?
Where is the noise without the silent?
Where is democracy without the tyrant?
Where is the foe without the friend?
Where is the start without the end?

Stephen A Owen

 Ever since a young age, I have always been interested in writing, whether it is short stories, verses or even letters. From there, it went to reading poetry. I realised I could write short poems too. I didn't take it seriously, people would tell me the poems were very good. One day I sent a poem titled 'Me 'N' Jesus' to a publisher's advertising for budding poets. That was my first ever poem published. From then on I have had many more published in anthologies.

I tend to write about life experiences. Being influenced by a big family and growing up in a city that had fell to recession. In a bleak 80's era. Poverty and depression in a rundown place. Liverpool was a dirty, deprived city. Buildings in desperate need of a makeover and the docks, they were busy but the Mersey polluted with oil and debris. However, the people made up for it, survivors, with the humour that came with it. A Scouser will always see the funny side to anything.

Influences in my life have been my parents, George and Lily, then sisters and brothers, Karen, Sandra, John and Lennie. And my own sons Karl and Mark too, I love you all. Aunties and uncles, lots of cousins and nephews and nieces, that is how it was in those days I guess, big families.

I do write a lot about certain themes. My hometown for one, my family, Sept 11, but mostly I like to write about the sea and the countryside. There is something special and magical about the waves crashing onto the shore. Or the grass and the trees blowing in the breeze on a summer's day, nature at its best.

When I am not writing I enjoy listening to music, all kinds. I play and watch football. Playing the drums too, it is so relaxing. Or take a brisk walk along the beach on a cold, windy day with the rain on my face and the waves white and raging.

So that is about it, a brief description of me, I hope you enjoy reading my poems as much as I enjoy writing. These poems were chosen for me. If certain people feel left out I apologise, no harm was intended.

My Aunty, My Special Lady

(In memory of Aunty May)

From the depths of the Mersey across the Ocean
into America so many years ago
you were always my favourite aunty
because you lived so far away
too far for me as a snotty-nosed kid
to come to visit you and stay
as you know it was impossible in them days
it was hard because I loved you Aunty May

Even though I was the last one to get to know you
being the baby of the bunch
I wish I could have come to see you
take you and Uncle Hugh out to lunch
I think I was nine
I loved Belton Road around that time
my memories of you were special ones
we lived round the corner from Aunty Winnie
and Uncle John's.
The place I grew up and thought up all of my goals
I never made it as a fireman
but I did get rid of my snotty nose.

What I did achieve was nothing to be proud of
but what I got was a loving family
and two healthy sons
parents I love so dearly
and sisters and brothers too
but who needs dreams
when they don't come true
when there are special people in this world
just like you.

Why is life so cruel
to the ones who mean so much to me
why was it cruel to you
now you are no longer here
I will always remember you
my Aunty, my special lady.

This Is A Tribute

This is a tribute
to my dad and mum
two people in my life
that mean more to me than anyone

This is a tribute
to my sisters and brothers
who are themselves fathers and mothers
also to their own children too
this is going out also to you

This is a tribute
to my own son Karl
and my stepson Mark too
I miss you both so much
love and hugs to you
these holiday times are when I miss you
this is a special one for you

This is a tribute to whoever I have missed out
love to you and a great big shout out
so many to mention but you know who you are
this is a tribute to the special people in my life
I love you all by far

But most of all this is a tribute
for all mankind
and for the ones who went to war
came home heroes
injured
paralysed
even blind
helping to build a better place for this damn race
hope it was worth the blood and tears
and you aren't haunted by what you saw
for so many years.

Make Me Feel Six Feet Tall

(Dedicated to my mum)

I watch you and I smile
Your expressions say it all
You always give me a smile
Make me feel six feet tall
Never thought I would feel
So close to you again
I always thought we grow
And things are never the same

Spending this time with you
Has made me feel real again
And if I could only give to you
What you need to feel the same

I love you because you are my mum
However, to me you are a little bit more
A friend when I need you the most
Your support I have that is for sure

All I ask is you take care of yourself
Do not do too much, excel yourself
And we will have many happy times to come
I'm so happy I have you as my mum.

Guess It's Just Another Autumn Breeze

Leaves are falling off the trees
Weather's changing
Another autumn breeze
Squirrels are stocking up
Say goodbye to the buttercup
Farmers have worked hard to plough the land
Traces of summer holidays remain on the sand

It's a breezy day today
Another breezy day tomorrow
Deckchair man counts his loss
And drowns away his sorrow
But there's a nice thing about autumn
Sunsets are oh so bright
People wrapped up, stroll through the park
Getting ready for a chilly night

The rain has started to fall
As the squirrel hides away in the village hall
Waiting for the rain to end
Cleaning his paws
Rain dripping from his coat
Grey in colour
Red patch round his throat
When the rain stops falling
The mother squirrel is heard in the distance calling
Father leaves the hall and gathers up his stash
The puddles from the shower leave a dampened and muddy path

There's a chill in the air
A dampness about the place
A man walks his dog
He has a wind and rain-soaked face
Struggles with the umbrella he holds tight in his hand
His dog thinks he wants to play
The mutt don't understand
The man pulls at the dog's lead
Playfully the dog thinks it's time for a feed
When the man shouts down to the hound
No need the dog thinks
And lays on the ground.

Still there's a chill and soon it will freeze
Guess it's just another autumn breeze.

Dad I Want To Thank You

(Dedicated to my dad)

I grew up in a tough world
But in my dad's world
He taught me to be strong
Be kind to people
Be sure to listen well
And to try your best to love everyone
My dad has always been there for me
I've put him at the top of my family tree

As a boy
I was only interested in playing with toys
Football after school
Breaking all my parents' rules
Didn't have much time to spend with my dad
Not that I didn't care
I was far too busy being a kid somewhere

I remember waiting at the gate for him to return from work
He'd always have a treat for me
Being the youngest of five
Guess it was my little perk
He'd spend hours teaching me to play the guitar
Didn't have time for a remote-controlled car

All my life I don't think I told him
Just how much he means to me
Cos it's something us men forget to do
It doesn't come so easily
Saying how much I love you
I think my dad is great
More than that he's me mate
Now I'm a man myself Dad
All I have I owe to you
Now I have my own world
Dad I want to thank you . . .

Always Be Your Kid

(For my brother John written after a holiday in Florida)

Saying goodbye to you
Made it clear to me
No matter who we are in life
Where would we be without our family
And even though sometimes
We may not get it right
An occasional argument
Please let's never fight

Life's too short
To end the way we nearly did
You're my big brother
I'll always be your 'kid'
Now that you have gone
I feel lost and alone
Can't wait to hear from you
Safe and sound from your home

We've had such a good time
In all that we did
Fishing in the river
Like when we were kids
Brothers in arms
We'll get closer from this
Forget the bad times
Forgive me if I made you annoyed

Brother I love you mate
Even though sometimes
In my face there is hate
Respect for you I have again
Me on the outside I act a clown
On the inside there is pain and a frown.

I Won't Feel So Alone

(Dedicated to Sandra's love for Kimberley)

I was looking through some photographs today
a nice surprise in front of me
was a picture of you staring at me
made me feel so happy
were my dreams gonna come true?
It was Christmas morning
and you were opening your presents
you were so happy
like an angel sent down from Heaven
as I sat there on my own
I wanted so much to telephone
but I know right now you don't seem to care
you have a new life now somewhere

Do you still think of me?
Do you miss your family?
Do you remember the times that we shared?
Do you feel sad, do you still care?
Because I think of you every day
in a motherly kind of way
I've tried so hard
and I can't get you out of my mind
I'm so worried about you
feels like I'm going out of my mind

I wish I could turn back the clock
to see if we could change things
maybe we'd take a different route this time
stay away from all those bad times
if you are not happy in your new home
please come back to me, make me smile again
don't leave me alone on your doorstep
getting cold and getting wet.

I'm your mum, you are still my little girl
can't we be friends, can't I be part of your world?
Give it time and when you want to come home
just pick up the phone and I won't feel so alone . . .

That's All I Need

(Dedicated to old Bill laying in his hospital bed)

She visits me and talks to me every day
She talks to me but I've got nothing to say
She takes my temperature
She wipes my brow
I've got so much to say to her
But I don't know how
My dignity has been taken from me
I can't wash myself
Can't even take myself to the lavatory
I wear a pad as if that's not enough
She takes it to the sleuce to get rid of the stuff
I stare at her in my silent world
My body has twisted and my bones have curled
24/7 I need her care
In my lonely world all I can manage is a stare
She feeds me, bathes me, takes care of my needs
But I have my life that's all I need.

Her Last Words To Jake Before She Died

Ground Zero
anniversary two years old
many questions still unanswered
different stories still getting told
looking around the place
the agony still etched on a family's face

A banner reading 'I really miss you Mom'
holding it high and proud
is her sad and lonely twelve-year-old son
at the age of ten
she kissed him goodbye
'Don't be late for school'
her last words to Jake before she died
he stands on his own
quietly he cries
his dad takes a handkerchief and wipes the tears
from his eyes

It's a day
again the whole world will never forget
it brings back the pain
the memories and the death
it's a time to hug and a time to show
that the feelings are getting stronger
that love will never go

A flower stands alone
in the dirt of Ground Zero
was planted in rememberance
two years ago
it blooms today for all to see
dedicated to the lost souls
in loving memory

God bless you
we are all thinking of you . . .

Caron P Simpson

After leaving school I trained as a nursery nurse, then I went to Braford College and trained as a nursery and infant teacher. I then got married, and worked in Blackburn as a nursery teacher before starting a family.

I started to write when I had a young family and we owned a bookshop. Unfortunately my marriage collapsed because of illness. I am now in my forties and am a volunteer helper in a charity shop. I also go to various craft classes where I do decoupage, card marking, patchwork and quilting, embroidery, tapestry and soft furnishings.

True Worship

Come and bow down before You Lord.
Because You are good and kind.
We worship and adore You
As we were designed to do this.
Let's have true intimacy with You O God,
Help us to put You first,
So will receive so much more,
Give us a hunger and thirst
That only You can satisfy.
Praise the Lord in Zion.
Thank Him for He is the King of Kings
And Lord of Lords
His love is eternal.

The Beauty Of God

As our minds
Ponder on loving God
We can feel His presence
Through the warmth of a lovely atmosphere
And as we lift our hearts to Him
Concentrating on His sovereignty
The risen Lord
Seated in Heavenly realms
Where the angels are dancing
Around His golden throne
Singing Psalms of exaltation
Seeing the glory of Christ!

Prayer

Into Your presence O Lord, I come
And put my requests unto You.
Seeking Your wonderful face.
Knowing that the door will be opened unto me,
Lord, have Your way I ask
And let me have completeness
That You alone are everything to me.
In You I trust
And have sweet fellowship
Having a conversation with You
In seeking your will
Lord, live in my heart
Let Your will be done.

Looking Beyond . . .

When life seems an uphill struggle,
And that's the way it feels sometimes,
May my hope be in the Lord Jesus Christ,
Who will carry me through
The darkness of night,
To shelter under his wing
And be protected until the light flickers through.

What Do We Believe?

There are ways we can receive from God.
His blessings we have day by day.
God has lavished on us His incredible way.
We have a big and wonderful God.
Along His mighty path we travel,
Where we can wear the crown of righteousness
And put our faith in action.

A Treasure Chest

God's promises are rich beyond measure,
When we open the bible of treasure.
He tells us how we should live,
Then shows me how to forgive.
So dear God, when I look unto you each day,
Help me walk on life's pathway.
Then I may receive
The blessings when I believe.
Your goodness that dwells
Richly in my heart,
To give me a brand new start,
Forgetting the past.
And my burdens I can cast
A rainbow is in sight,
So I can be happy and bright.

Bible Thoughts

A treasure chest of promises,
Are sent from Heaven above,
For those who faithfully trust,
In Christ's redemptive love.

Eternal Security Of The Believer

Can I come back to You Lord,
If I fall away from You?
After being in the light and receiving the Holy spirit.
Please Lord,
Restore my salvation and bring back the joy of the Lord.
Help me not to be back slidden,
But be married unto You.
So I'm not getting a divorce.
I'm trusting You Lord completely for the rest of my days.

The Sun Is Shining Through

Amongst the turmoil of life,
It seems like there is an overwhelming darkness
Where nothing seems to be going right,
We have to hold onto the love of God,
That He will bring us through these times,
Then like the middle of winter, it suddenly turns into spring.
Where we can experience the warmth and sunlight it offers.
Let us never lose sight of Jesus
So we can rest in His presence.

Spring

It's the time of year
When nature starts to wake up.
The daffodils and primroses are in our gardens.
Lambs skip in the fields.
Buds come on the trees.
The birds sing some little tunes,
A reawakening of nature.
When we can see God's goodness
Come alive before our eyes.
There is a feeling of expectancy in the air
So we can put away our sorrows and cares
And be cheerful.

A Breath Of Fresh Air

In life's business
Isn't it nice
To stand still
And look around
At everything we see
Perhaps a scenic view
With undulating countryside and hills in the distance
So let's ponder . . .
And perhaps sit by the stream
Watching water trickling over the stones
The primroses arranged in clusters on the banking
A rainbow in the distance
With small droplets of rain coming from the sky
Are the times we can feel the depth of God's richness -
In His creation we can see His hand.

Easter

The blades of grass blow in the breeze.
The little flowers stand like soldiers,
Dignified and self-surviving,
Where the clouds rise above
And the cross in the distance
Is where Jesus died for us.
With His blood, our sins He bore,
So we can have eternal life.
The darkness is changing into light.
Where once we were lost, we can now appreciate
The hope we have been given
Through the events of Easter time.

The Cross

As Jesus went to the cross
At Easter
He had nails driven through Him,
His body must have suffered.
Was it physical
When those scars were shown
Or was it the fact
That he was despised
And rejected by man?
His strong belief
Showed us light
He died, so . . .
We can be saved in His grace
This Easter time.

A Pot Of Gold

There is a rainbow in the sky,
Shadowing through the clouds.
A beautiful bunch of flowers
Portraying the colours of the rainbow
Arranged in a church window.

Sometimes we may have a dark cloud over our lives,
And blackness surrounds our thinking,
Then Jesus may say,
'Come on, and look beyond,
I can see some beautiful colours.
A reminder of God's love'.

The rainbow is in sight, where the sun starts to shine through.
The glimmer changes into a ray of sunshine,
And we will be like the flowers in the field blowing in the breeze.

Patchwork Quilt

The fields
As they display
Different greens
With clusters of
Trees around . . .
The fencing,
Like a running stitch,
Encloses the various units.
A dark patch is where the ploughing has been,
Then the purple field of heather is at the top of the hill,
Giving a varied texture
To thank God for His goodness
And His majestic love.

Belief In Jesus

I'm often reminded of Jesus
When I look at the wonder of creation.
Those hills in the distance
With the trees dotted around
And the gardens with colourful flowers in them.
Those narrow country lanes
Where the animals are dreamily grazing in the fields
And the trickling of a brook
As the water flows over the stones.

To turn my back
On such a tranquil setting
Would be likened to sitting in a dark room,
So I'm keeping my door open
And letting the light of Jesus shine through,
Then His love
Will help me on life's way.

Reflections

Sitting on a barge,
Travelling along,
Seeing beautiful scenery,
As the sun shines through the woodland,
And the cows, grazing in the green fields.
The gentle breeze is on my face.
So we see God's handiwork,
The strengths of His character.
Each little bridge we go through
Claims just another part of our journey,
Where we can venture into new territory,
With Jesus as our guide.

In God's Beautiful Garden

There are trees snuggled in the hills
Portraying a green array.
Ducks waddling around the pond,
Goats, sheep and cows grazing in the fields.
Settlements have been built amongst it,
With flower beds and rockeries in and around.
The butterflies dance among the flowers,
While the bees scurry amongst the pollen.
The luscious countryside
With the trickling brook
And tweeting birds,
And the squirrels starting to rush around for nuts.
So such is summer when it is turning to autumn.

Jugging Along

Is life an uphill struggle
Or is it just fine
When jugging along
On an old steam train
Through the trees of the forest
With the light of the sun
Refracting on the leaves
Showing the browns, reds, yellows and greens
Reaching middle age
And experiencing different encounters
I hope a stage of maturity.

The Way Ahead

Seasons come and seasons go.
The buds turn to leaves and then they fall bare.
Life goes on
Through the calms and the storms.
We can't see what the future holds,
Only that we must look to Jesus,
Take hold of His hand
And walk the pathway he has chosen.
The sun shines, the rain pours and gusts of wind may be strong at times,
Then when it is cold and frosty, layers of clothes cover our bodies.
I ask myself, *what am I?*
Does my personality change with the seasons?
Is my life like the weather?
The path may not always look straight and there may be bends
But then, like a stone exposed to the elements,
The roughness changes into a smooth surface.
Does God expose our erosion to upgrade His design for us?
'I hope so.'

The Storms Of Life

Who can this be?
Yes, His name was Jesus.
After working all day, teaching the crowds
He got into a boat with His disciples.
There was a violent storm and the disciples started to panic
As you would.
Meanwhile, Jesus was sleeping,
So they woke Him up.
Jesus was in control of the storm
Because He was God's son.
Are we in that boat,
Facing lots of different storms of life?
It may be sickness, bereavement, unemployment or divorce.
Remember folks, lean on the Lord and trust in Him
Then the sea will become calm.

Ian McCrae

I was born in Romford in Essex, the youngest of three children, and lived in that area until I married in 1967. After several work related moves, I came to Suffolk in 1979 with my pregnant wife and two sons. The newcomer turned out to be a daughter. My continued residence in Suffolk has, unfortunately, outlasted my marriage and, of my family, just my eldest son, my daughter and a grandson remain in the county.

Rapidly approaching my sixtieth birthday, I have had a varied career, ranging from shop management to taxi driving and signwriting to meter reading. However, a large part of my working life has involved me in dealing directly with people from almost every walk of life.

I currently work as a barman in a busy public house in Needham Market. It was here that, about a year ago, I started to entertain the customers with humorous poems about some of the characters amongst them. Behind the bar is a perfect place to learn what goes on in people's minds and in their lives. After a drink or two they will tell you their troubles or regale you with amazing anecdotes.

The subject matter of my poems broadened to cover human nature and relationships in general, partly from personal experience and partly from observation of others, but the response from the regular drinkers remained enthusiastic and I eventually took a deep breath and submitted some poems for publication. I was, and still am, surprised to find that several have been accepted.

A Poem Of Little Value

Some are born to happiness
And others, they are not.
They live their lives in twilight
And must accept their lot.
They have their days of gaiety
And weeks of feeling blue,
They don't believe they're worth much
No matter what they do.
They drive off those who love them
But don't know the reason why,
They are victims of depression
And they fail before they try.

Aftermath

So, now that it's all over,
Now we've fought our war,
Now we've torn each other
To shreds with tooth and claw,
There're little bits of broken heart
Lying on the floor
And tattered threads of worn-out love
Blowing out the door.
Was it all a waste of time?
I just can't say for sure,
Perhaps I may know better
When the wounds are not so raw.

Beauty And The Beast

You really put me off my stroke
With your laughing eyes.
I thought that you might want me,
But wishes tell such lies.

You're so youthful, full of life
So you can pick and choose,
I'm old and battered, lacking shine
Like a well-worn pair of shoes.

You're attractive and you're fun,
You, any man might love,
But we're no more akin, we two,
Than a buzzard and a dove.

The story of Beauty and the Beast
Came to a happy conclusion,
But fairy tales are not real life,
They're just daydreams and illusion.

Folk Song

Some folk have lots of money which they like to flash about;
Some folk work hard all their lives and end up owning nowt.
Some folk are quite saintly and some are very bad;
Some folk are always happy and some are always sad.

Some folk never seem to get their just desert;
Some folk always seem to end up getting hurt.
There may not be much justice in this world of ourn
But any road you mustn't let it get you down.

Some folk are very 'umble, some are awfully grand,
Some are bitter, some are sweet and some are rather bland.
Some folk give out orders while others work and slave,
But they'll all be much the same when they're in the grave.

Guess Who

There's someone who I like a lot,
Someone I adore.
There's someone I'd miss very much
If she showed me the door.
There's someone who is very sweet,
Someone who is dear,
Someone who, I pray to God,
Will evermore be near.

There's someone who'll always love you,
To whose heart you hold the key,
And if you don't already know it . . .
That someone is me.

Home Feet

Apart from the rain, it's beautiful weather.
Home, feet, and don't spare the leather.
Heading for bed at five in the morning,
Already another grand day is dawning.
I don't care that my friends say my goose is cooked,
I've known for some time now that she's got me hooked.
But I'm walking home feeling light as a feather,
So home, feet, and don't spare the leather.

It's a lovely night, I'm at the start of my tether.
Home, feet, and don't spare the leather.
Don't mess around, feet, will you behave?
People are sleeping, it's quiet as the grave.
Will you stop dancing and get on with the walking?
If anyone sees us they'll all soon be talking
About the all time me and she spend together.
So home, feet, and don't spare the leather.

I've got no worries though I've lost my lucky heather,
Home, feet, and don't spare the leather.
I ought to care that the rent is due;
How I'm going to pay it, I haven't a clue,
But a certain pretty face and pair of bright eyes
Have got me convinced I'm wealthy and wise.
There's nothing I can't do with a little endeavour,
So home, feet, and don't spare the leather.

If You Want To Be My Friend

I wonder if you like me or just don't give a jot,
Some days you're my friend, some days you're not.
Some days you blow hot and some days you're cool,
You seem to think I'm some kind of fool.

One day you'll come calling, wanting me to play
But you'll be disappointed to find I've gone away.
If you never want to let me share your toys
Don't think I'll share you with other boys.

You won't play hopscotch, you won't play ball
And I don't find you any fun at all.
You're always busy, won't talk when I phone,
So don't think I'll be sorry when you're all alone.

When no one wants you, you'll pout and cry,
You'll come to my door heaving a sigh,
But I'll be too busy, I won't play your games,
Then you'll be sorry that you called me names.

Still, I don't bear grudges, I can forgive,
Show me you're sorry and together we'll live
In a pretty cottage down by the sea
Where we'll play forever, just you and me.

It's Being So Cheerful

Today's been pretty awful,
But, likely, tomorrow will be worse.
The train was late coming home,
You should have heard the missus curse.

'Your dinner's in the oven!
It'll be burnt to a frazzle now!'
You know, I sometimes wonder
Why I married the mis'rable cow.

They forecast, rain tomorrow,
And gale force winds as well.
There'll be no summer this year
As far as I can tell.

There's more repeats on telly,
That's all they're ever showing.
I wonder, sometimes, we don't give up.
I s'pose being cheerful keeps us going.

Just A Small Glass

'Give me a whisky, please, barman . . .
Or perhaps you should make it a double . . .
And, please, just a small splash of water,
You see, I've got woman trouble.

Like they say, there's no living with 'em
And without them you may's well be dead.
Perhaps I should give up living.'
'Oh, I wouldn't do that, Sir,' I said.

'People like you are important,
You help to keep me in a job.'
He gave a wry smile without meeting my eye
And a laugh, or was it a sob?

'Being alone, Sir, isn't really so bad.
The first ten years are the worst.
Take me, I've been on my own for so long
That in love I think I am cursed.'

'Give me a whisky, please, barman,
And perhaps you should have one yourself.'
'Thank you, I don't mind if I do, Sir.'
And I took another small glass from the shelf.

Ninety-Three, Not Out

(For Vera, who mocks all fears of growing old)

A little drop of whisky
Does no one any harm
And poured into a cup of tea
It adds a certain charm.
When you're ninety-three
It's no time to give things up,
So never mind what Matron says,
Please put a wee dram in my cup.

Round And Round

See the baby girl so tiny
Hair so black, eyes big and shiny;
See her learning how to smile,
Starting to learn how to beguile.

See the small girl with her toys,
See her tears and see her joys.
Feel the way she fills your heart;
She'll never from your thoughts depart.

See her grow, childhood can't linger,
But she still turns you round her finger.
How you fuss and how you worry
As off to meet some boy she'll hurry.

See the baby, safe from harm,
Cradled by your daughter's arm,
Soon to know life's joys and woes;
See the circle turn and close.

As the generations grow,
Round and round the circles go,
Always turning, never still,
Nothing ends, it never will.

Teenage Chaos

There're knickers hanging from the lamp
And bras upon the floor,
The telephone bill has doubled
And there're boys at every door.
You can't get in the bathroom
No matter how you try.
The teenager daughter's home again,
The house is like a sty.
The stereo is throbbing
Your head is like to burst;
Do you want her home or far away?
You can't think which is worst.

'Have you missed me, Dad?'
She cries as she bursts in.
'Of course I've missed you, baby;
It's been tidy and no din.'
She pulls a face, sticks out her tongue,
Leaves her bags to block the hall
And everything seems normal,
As if she'd not been gone at all.

The Crack Of Doom

Oh, those eyes, magnetic eyes,
That drew me on and on
And brought our flesh together
In a passion, now all gone.

Oh, those lips, such honeyed lips,
That caused my lips to burn
And my cold heart to smoulder
And still to sadly yearn.

Oh, those arms, those tender arms,
Enfolded me so nearly;
I fought to keep myself and soul
And won, but, oh, so dearly.

Oh, that love, that too fierce love,
That love that couldn't bend,
Was doomed from the beginning
To stress, to crack, to end.

The End Of Love

Rain clouds gather overhead,
The sky takes on the hue of lead.
'Woe is me,' the traveller said,
'The spirit of love is wholly dead.'

Underfoot the sod is cold,
The lambs are missing from the fold.
Mournfully, the bell is tolled
For hope that finally loses hold.

'Whither now?' the traveller cries,
Seeking truth and hearing lies,
'Take me to a man who's wise
That I may beg him to advise.'

Alas, no wise man can be found
Though the traveller's pleas abound.
In the dark is heard no sound
But the distant baying of a hound.

The Hermit

There's a little hermit crab
Living in a shell,
Imprisoned there by Doubt and Fear
Who cast a wicked spell.
Some day Light and Knowledge
Will break into her cell
And rescue her from Dark Despair,
Then in the sun she'll dwell.

The Market Café

There's a café by the market;
It's been there for years;
Chrome and vinyl for easy cleaning,
Staffed by little dears.
Half a dozen conversations
Are mingling in my ears
As I sit and soak up coffee
And bottle up my tears.
They don't charge for being cheerful
That's free - part of the deal -
So when I'm feeling down and crushed
And broken on life's wheel
I pop into the café
For a cuppa and a meal.

The Old Man And The Young Man

The young man mocked the old man
Because he'd lost his youth,
But the old man smiled in sympathy
And said, 'I'll tell a truth:
I have stood where you stand,
But can you surely say
That you will stand where I stand
On some future day.'

To The Ladies . . .

The reunion dinner was a success,
Though every year attendance grows less.
'To the ladies' the colonel proposed they drink,
Then turning to Standish he gave a wink.

'I'm rather fond of the ladies,
But there are very few about -
Lots of Valkyries from Hades
Who push and swear and shout.

Where are the maidens, so demure,
Today it seems they are much fewer.
I suppose modern girls aren't *bad*, though bold -
It's just that I've grown damnably old.'

Sharon Louise de Klerk

When I was 11 years old, my family and I moved from Hertfordshire to a small village in Lincolnshire. I remember feeling extremely bewildered and lonely and it was very difficult adjusting to the difference in school systems. Because of this and my extreme shyness I spent a lot of time on my own.

I loved music and so began writing song lyrics and reading poetry often as a way of putting my feelings down on paper and finding solace in poets' words. Since then my interest in poetry, both reading and writing has escalated, the former often providing inspiration for my own work.

I particularly enjoyed my time at university doing an English degree as I could indulge my hobby while also receiving invaluable advice, feedback and encouragement from the tutors.

My ideas can come from any source: something someone says, a piece of music, people I meet, an interesting word or phrase, sometimes the smallest of things can be a catalyst for writing a poem. For example, my love of sweets gave me the idea for 'Day Trip To The Sweet Shop'. I am very close to my family, especially my mother and so I tend to write poems around this theme. I also like writing poems for greetings cards and as gifts for family and friends.

I love the whole process of writing a poem, from the initial idea, the first line, whether it takes one draft or many, through to the final poem and thinking of a title.

Generation Gap

In the bedroom
An untuned transistor flickers; bald tyres on gravel
A phantom transmits its subtle spell

On the cardboard mattress, the gritty shell
From an old man's last meal
Stings his throat, chokes him

His gurgles just audible above the
Screeching stereo and screaming tyres

A stone's throw away
The young man grits his teeth
The heat hovers above his head

Drying the throat, grilling each gasp
Before him the hot house slowly steams
The garrotte tightens its grip

It is only curiosity that fuels his step
Not love or kindness or even
Hatred but an

Unkept promise; father to son

The glass is all cracks and cobwebs
The stairway crumbles like eggshells underfoot
Undeterred the young man

Advances upon the rotting wood
He reaches the rest room and
Hears the crash, the transistor

Crackles, cuts
Crackles, cuts out

The garbled gasping of the old man
Flakes, flags
Flakes, flags out

He just caught the old man's
Last dying breath
He tried to keep hold of it, but
The heat had reached boiling point
And he lost his footing . . .

Pity; but they never were on the same wavelength

Empty Matchbox

He looked just like a matchstick man,
My dad
His legs; flagpoles
His trousers; flags
He looked as though he should have been in a painting,
Ceremoniously standing
Amongst the cats and dogs

And it was raining that day. The last time I saw him

The day I saw his tears,
So sharp
They splintered all our lives

The day
Frightened cats ran from my eyes,
And the dogs
With all their ferocity,
Were too slow to catch them up

Even now,
Your face
Loosely holding the last fragments
Of flesh,
Fills my mind

It's funny
Now

But as a child I drew you as a matchstick
Dad
With my matchstick pets and matchstick
Mum
I even used a matchstick to draw a curved
Sun

> But, you used those matchsticks
> To light your cigarettes,
> And the smoke covered my curved sun
> Until nothing remained of my picture.

Wake To Breathe

Your tired eyes need to wake to blue skies
Your lonely heart needs to rest in open arms
Your idle hands need to touch on tender skin
All your senses should be involved in;
The beautiful day

Your quiet mouth needs to speak loving words
Your ears need to hear softly spoken replies
You need so much to see someone smile
And kiss the sorrow from your beautiful eyes

Your head needs to be held as high as the sky
Your feet need to walk in step with another
Your skin needs to feel the warmth of soft kisses
Your body needs to lay down next to a lover

And I wish that your eyes could wake up smiling
And see only beauty in all of your day
So your tired heart beneath static skin
Could wake to breathe and
Beat again.

Progress

You went through so much to get your tattoo,
Despite the pain you had
        to gain my mark, my name
Now it's over, I have changed.

Remote Control

I want you to sit with me in my garden
When the sun shines down so lovely
I want you to sit with me in my lonely kitchen
And share a cup of tea
I want you to sit down for a little while
On my 2 seater settee
I want to fight over the remote
While we watch Friday night TV

I want you to walk down my crazy paving
And knock at my front door
I want you to sit down at my table
And leave muddy marks on my clean floor
I want you to share my TV dinners and then
Argue over the washing up
I want to see your face turn angry red
When I break another cup

I want to sit on the back row at the movies
And hold your clammy hand
I want to fight over the last pick 'n' mix
At the bottom of the bag
And when we're walking to the bus stop
I want to wear your winter fleece
I want to put my hand in your back pocket
While we're walking down the street

I want to whisper in your ear
While you pretend I never spoke
I want to tell you something funny
And hear you laugh at the marvellous joke
I want to hide your pack of fags
When you want to have a smoke
I want to hear your jealous ravings
When I look at another bloke

But
Most of all I want you
To step back into your role
Take up your old position
And give me back some
Remote
Control

Because now you are not with me
I have nothing substantial left
And I hope it's not true what my mother said
That
'Those who want just don't get!'

Day Trip To The Sweet Shop

She waltzes in; a whirl of flesh
With sweaty palms and shining smile
     The slippery 50p; a winged god
                         to the watery mouths
                         at the misty window,
                         huddled tightly
                         standing on tiptoe.

     She can't believe her eyes
     But her mouth cannot mimic her mind

     In plastic cases and cardboard boxes
Towering jars and wicker baskets
     Raspberry reds, banana yellows, marshmallow
pinks and plum blues. A mountain of mini
     marvels:
Beautiful bracelets worn like jewels
     Carefully carved chocolate shaped like tools
Sticky toffee that numbs the teeth
     Glues the gums and stifles speech
Slinky sherbet that tingles the tongue
     Slides down slowly and lasts as long as the
Strawberry shoelaces and liquorice pipes
     Everything Mummy and Daddy dislikes!

An assortment of Allsorts and one penny to be spent

     So, with flushed cheek she takes her pick
To line her paper bag with the brilliant plumage
     Each feather picked with precision
She makes her final decision; the misty mouths
                         at the watery window
                         hold their breath,
                         they only just see
                         the winged 50p
                         slide onto the shelf

     And out she whirls

The trail from the tardis trickles behind
  following her flighty feet
Lasting until she swallows her last
  savoured sweet

And the misty-eyed mother
Thinks of the link
That binds them both together
Like slinky sherbet
that tingles the tongue and
lasts as long as the
feather.

Mothering

Mother, I see your eyes are wrung
Out. Your
Tear-stained tea towel
Has bared its threads
Everything topples too soon. Take a
Rest.

The Long Goodbye

I loved to lay and watch you wake
And see the sleep still in your eyes
To hold your hand
And kiss your fingers
Soft like gentle lullabies

I loved to sit and watch you smoke
To see you think and dream a while
I loved the way your lips looked
When a happy memory made you smile

I loved to stand and watch you talk
To see the way your mouth moved
I loved to hear your favourite thoughts
Your lovely voice could always soothe

I loved to walk in step with you
And hear your foot fall next to mine
To feel the warmth from your beautiful body
Breathe my own back into life

But

I hated to see the back of you
When I stood to see you turn and go
And I hope one day I'll be able to say
You were just a man I used to know.

Photo From A Family Album

Your sunken eyes
Stare at me
From the sad photograph
As if threatening to jump from the sockets
If I look long enough

From a distance it looks like
You are smiling, but
You don't know what your
Next-door neighbour is doing

Until the evidence is exposed. And the camera never lies

I used to despise
Those uncaring people
Who
    Hear but don't listen
Who
    Look but don't see
But
    Obviously that was me

I'm sorry I didn't see
You were sad,
Even with the negative in my empty hand
I still don't believe
So, I'll keep you on the mantelpiece

In your gilt frame,
And from the farthest corner of the room
All I will see is your slight smile
And imagine you are laughing.

After Word

Where are you?
I wish I knew,
So when I think of you
I can picture you in the proper place

Are you faraway, floating
In the freezing sky
Dreamily drifting among the lazy clouds?
Are you in the crumble of leaves
Beneath clumsy boots, the dead grass
Beneath the grazing cows?

Where are you?
I wish I could see,
I wish you would show your face
To me

Are you sailing somewhere
In the silent sea
Drifting through the whispering waves?
Are you in the fresh April flowers that
Grow in the park to brighten up the
Dull spring days?

Where are you?
I wish I knew,
So when I think of you
I can picture your body, your face

I wonder

Are you the shadow that shades the summer sun
The last of the light that filters through?
You must be hiding somewhere
There must be something left of you . . .

Jean Bagshaw

Educated at Scholey Hill Primary School, Methley; Wakefield Girls' High School; the North of England Secretarial College, Leeds; Leeds Polytechnic and the Open University.

I have a BA Hons in European Humanities with English and a City and Guilds' Teachers' Certificate in Further Education. I taught, part-time, in adult education for 20 years. I am now retired and suffer from Multiple Sclerosis.

I was born into a farming family in 1941 and have lived on a farm all my life. I have been married for 40 years to my farmer husband and we have 2 married sons and 5 grandchildren.

I became interested in poetry whilst covering a creative writing group for a sick colleague 12 years ago.

Happenings in everyday life such as the elements, places, nature and people inspire my writing. I also find the use of language fascinating.

My hobbies are swimming, crosswords, reading, listening to classical music, painting, visiting antique fairs, history and writing. I am currently trying to write my first novel which is set, of course, on a Yorkshire farm.

A Silent Intruder

Feather-like, floating, falling,
Gently swirling, twirling,
Glistening, shimmering starlets,
Pureness, whiteness, tiny-ice lets.

Silently landing, covering, blanketing,
Smothering, shrouding, hiding,
In virgin cloak a silver wilderness,
Reforming, strange and eerie stillness.

Intrudes all forms disfiguring,
Camouflaging, deeply drifting,
Unheard, the world disguised,
All of nature now transformed.

Hope Out Of The Dark

How bleak and sallow wintry days,
The sun an orb of watery glaze,
Blow bitter winds and icy showers,
Sharp tentacles, invasive powers.

Sure, swift to penetrate - to petrify -
all living creatures doomed to die,
Come biting chill each bone is froze',
Each day at end before it 'rose.

Dark, dank and dull, there is no light,
No stars are seen as in the night,
An endless cold without relent,
Takes retribution - all seem spent.

But end they must these days of gloom
And out of dark the sun will come,
The earth with warmth will fill again,
Relieve each ache - release all pain,
Spring arises from the stark,
Bourne aloft with song of lark.

The Annual Renewal

Artists' palettes colours fresh,
Verdant, vibrant, vivid splash,
Birdsong, blossoms, bursting buds,
New nymphs flutter by pastures' sods.

Petals, sepals, leaves uncurl,
Softening breezes gently swirl,
Showers, shimmers, rainbow days,
Descended down through golden rays.

Brightness beams from bubbling brook,
Running, rippling through shady nook.
Silver shines on slippery scales,
On fishy fins and trouty tails.

Spirits soar on swallows' song -
Delighted, back from journeys long.
Nature now revived from dead,
Reborn - all blandness, bleakness shed.

To Greet The Spring

First to show - the aconite,
Golden petals, a shining light,
Around her neck wears ruff of green,
Deep-toothed leaves will last be seen.

Droopy snowdrop next appears,
Hangs white flower, sheds frozen tears.
Crocuses with buds rolled tight,
Bright in saffron, purple, white.

On sunny days they open wide,
Worker bees to seek inside -
the nectar they collect and store,
To fill the honeycomb once more.

Daffodils all nodding, golden,
Narcissus smile - cream petals open,
Trumpeting the start of spring,
Accompanies blackbirds as they sing.

Fleshy leaves 'round tulip flowers,
Cups of glowing, brilliant colours,
White and orange, purple, crimson,
Pointed, rounded, closed and open.

Irises of yellow, blues,
Spiky-leaved in greens subdued,
Flag and Orris, two to name,
In many hues but some the same.

Winter jasmine blossom leads,
Currants drip in pinks and reds,
Bare Daphne branches purple flowers,
Forsythia stars in golden showers.

All emerge from frozen earth,
Old Mother Nature giving birth,
Renews the life she'll always bring,
To bless us with her flowers of spring.

Halcyon Days

Soft and warm, long summer days,
Mornings bright with misty haze,
Dew enhances blossoms fair,
Heady perfume fills the air.

Sunbeam filters fleshy leaf,
Buzzing insects deftly weave -
Collecting pollen - nectar quest,
Fledglings falter from the nest.

Gentle colours blend to please,
Bodies soothed by cooling breeze,
Grasses tall on verges grow,
Maturing branches bending low.

Tiny fruits where blossoms grew,
Preparing seeds to grow anew,
Warmth and moisture - nature's aid -
The bounties for next season made.

The Elements
The Storm

Before it starts - all peace and calm,
Then, slowly builds the gathering storm,
First a breeze which then develops,
Into a wind which all envelops,
Builds momentum now becoming,
Tempest, torrent, terrifying.

Howls and whistles round the houses,
Buffets trees and plants and hedges,
Bending all that's in its path,
Punishing, subjugating wrath,
Swishes through the corners, cracks,
Mounting into bangs and whacks.

Crashes through all that's in its way,
Demolishes and stomps away,
Flattens, breaks and decimates,
And then the lull when it abates,
But only to regain its strength,
Begins again for a rebirth.

The rain joins in and drenches all,
Saturates and soaks in total,
Lashes against the windows, doors,
Propelled by fiercest force - it roars,
Uproots trees, breaks fences down,
Rages furiously 'til it's blown -
itself to pieces, then subsides,
Becoming slower, calmer, rides,
On gentler breezes - all receded,
Anger gone, the storm has ended.

The Wind

The wind blows free,
Across land and sea,
Blows ship and sail
And craft so frail,
Can be a friend,
In calm - God send.

The wind can blow,
Be gentle - flow,
Be soft-blown breeze,
Or gusts that seize -
A hat or leaf,
In heat - relief.

The wind can howl,
Be fierce and growl
Can whistle shrill,
Disturb the still,
Be freezing cold,
Chill young and old.

Can carry rain,
Beat on a pane,
Drift sleet and snow,
Makes noses glow,
Will damage roof
Freeze foot and hoof.

Wind whips up storms,
Distorts some forms,
With angry wrath,
All in its path.
Tosses objects all about,
Any lying in its route.

Brollies are turned inside out,
Banners flutter all about,
Dries the washing on the line,
Ripens grapes upon a vine,
Turns the harvest golden brown,
Nodding, swaying ears of corn.
Can make its way at many paces,
The wind can show such different faces.

A Housewife's Lament

Housework, housework what a chore,
Nothing but a great big bore,
Detesting all that endless dusting,
Hating most - the window cleaning.

Then there's vacuuming to be done,
Whoever said cleaning could be fun?
The interminable washing up -
Of plates and dishes, glass and cup.

The washing and the ironing too,
The whites and colours, whatever hue,
How I hate, dislike the chore,
Housework - one enormous bore.

Lots and lots of repetition,
Never finding the solution,
To the endless dirt and grime,
That finds its way into a home.

Mud galore from kids and dogs,
Cover carpets, floors and rugs,
Fingermarks all over paint,
Enough to make a housewife faint.

For evermore I'll have to slave,
How I wish that I could wave,
A magic wand to do it all,
So's I would never have to call -
'Housework, housework, what a bore,
Nothing but a great big chore.'

Halloween - Phantoms Of The Night

Moths flit, erratic to and fro,
Hither, thither, fluttering go,
Trying to capture evasive light,
Momentarily shining in the night.

Black, winged mice blindly fly,
Eerie, sinister passing by,
To join the images of the dark,
Threatening, frightening, grey and stark.

Faces peer from blackened trees,
Corpseless eyes evoking fears,
Whispers, shushes ghostly shadows,
Transparent figures on imagined gallows.

Cobwebs dangle to entrap,
Deadly, ready to enwrap,
Careless mortals, roaming souls,
Turned to spirits, lifeless ghouls.

Being A Mum

Being a mum means being there,
Whenever they need you - anywhere.

Wipe their tears when things go wrong,
Read at bedtime, sing a song,
Stick plasters onto cuts and grazes,
Put smiles back on little faces.

Sew on a button or darn a sock,
Repair a tear or make new frock,
Cook a meal and clean the clothes,
Wash their tiny hands and toes.

Hugs and kisses mend a lot,
Of little ailments that they've got,
Even when they grow - they need
Good old mum when need to feed.

They still bring dirty washing home,
Expect the ironing to be done,
Dinner to be on the table,
When they're bigger, grown and able.

They like to bring their friends to stay,
Any they meet along the way,
Girls and boys, no matter who,
Make room for all, we have to do.

They're always on the telephone,
Your home is really not your own,
The post, it seems, is always theirs,
When bills appear, they're always yours!

Pop and rock are played quite loudly,
And nothing's ever clean and tidy,
But when they go and live elsewhere,
It all seems empty - somewhat bare.

Yes, being a mum means being there,
Whenever they need you - anywhere.

Christmastime

The time of year we all adore,
Mistletoe hung by the door,
Christmas trees and fairy lights,
Crisp white frost on starry nights.
Chestnuts roasting in the hearth,
In the porch - a holly wreath.

Church is filled with joyful throng,
By lantern-light old carols sung,
Christ is born - we all rejoice,
Gathered here in happy voice.

Children sleeping peacefully,
Stockings hung up hopefully,
Happy smiles on faces lie,
Firelight flickers, embers die,
Requests are answered, dreams come true,
Stockings filled with parcels new.

Wrappings littered on the floor,
Chocolates, mince pies, food galore,
Lighted candles, ribbons red,
Turkey, stuffing; family fed,
Relaxing by the firelight glow,
Warm - away from cold and snow.

A Poem For Ann

I wish I'd told you when I could,
How grateful when you understood,
How much that laughter meant to me,
Your sound advice and sympathy.

I wish I'd spent more time with you -
To swap a story, point of view,
How much admired your astute mind,
An' aptitude for judgement, sound.

I wish that I could see you more,
Enjoy your knowledge, endless store
Of observations, balanced, fair,
Artistic talent, gift and flair.

I'm glad I knew you, valued friend,
The warmth I feel will never end.

Keith Leese

Keith Leese started writing poetry when he was about 18, producing some years later in 1983, a small book of his poems entitled 'Heaven Or Bust'. This work was never accepted for publication, subsequently his motivation, like his book, took something of a nose-dive. Despite writing numerous articles, short stories and in 1999 his autobiography, Keith wasn't to write poetry for the next 18 years.

A lifestyle change at the turn of the century, found Keith and his wife working for a public school in Dorset. One weekend at the end of the Michaelmas 2001 term, Keith, returning to school from the family home in Sussex, had been asked by his wife to bring with him a book of Christian poetry. His wife had been invited by the Housemaster to read a Christmas poem of her choice at house supper the following evening. Keith only remembered the book on the train back to Dorset. When scribing himself on this lapse, Keith writes, *I recall thinking, I'm a Christian poet*, so to save the day, 'Pictures Of Christmas' was written on a South West train between Sussex and Dorset.

This incident was to be the initial motivation for Keith to take up his pen and write poetry again, so after 18 years of silence the poet was reborn. Since then Keith has written over 50 poems, subjects as diverse as a forgotten World War I grave, to the comic antics of his dog, and of course new Christmas poems for 2002 and 2003.

This 4th compilation for Spotlight Poets, we journey with Keith back to his childhood in Kent, through his youth in the Baptist Church and into his early 20s. From this selection of poems, some from Keith's earliest work, we understand how life's primary experiences have shaped this poet. Keith's Christian faith has been the main driving force in his life since the age of 10. Consequently, faith and love are again prominent in this latest collection of poems, and like so much of Keith's work, are written in celebration of Him who gives us all whatever talents we have.

Revelation Three-Twenty

Why my Lord did You come to me then?
Too young to understand, just a boy of ten.
Child to youth I searched, Lord why my door,
why Lord You knocked, what in me You saw?
I sought to discover Your abundance, Your plenty,
my Damascus Road, I've found Revelation three-twenty.

Folkestone Harbour

I recall Folkestone harbour and the sea's call,
those gallant fishing boats coming home with their haul.
I miss the smell of the fish market and the sea foods,
I long for the sound of the ocean, in all its many moods.
I miss the noise of the seagulls and their hungry cry,
lest I forget those early days, as the years and miles go by.

First Love

First love must come to each young life,
Cupid's arrow, more like an assassin's knife.
Puppy love, friends say it's no big deal,
raw feelings, naked trust, nothing's so real.

First love's like a fever, an obsession of the mind,
you can't sleep, you can't study, first love is blind.
Too young to satisfy, too innocent to know why,
too inexperienced to understand, why first love must die.

Paperback Marxist

You tell me you have the answers you scholarly kid,
you tell of your philosophy, what Marx said and did.
You've read the paperback, you've seen a new truth,
another paperback Marxist, another hoodwinked youth.

Carbon copy psychology, another anarchist is bred,
one more victim to idealism, and not one hungry child fed.
Comrade, the revolution you seek is within the believer's call,
one Lord, one faith, and on this we all stand or fall.

Carey Baptist

I recall my days at Carey with great affection,
days of youth and learning, seeking our direction.
Eager to learn of Jesus, to feed our hunger,
to study the Word, to seek the truth and wonder.

Young and old we packed the Sunday meeting,
as Pastor Wilson delivered his steadfast teaching.
Believe and be baptised, a new truth we found,
a life call to service, in every good work to abound.

Heaven Or Bust

My friend, should you be called, as in time you must,
to answer who you serve, whether you're heaven or bust.
Should you be called to state just where you stand,
whether you'll cling to this life, or take His holy hand.

My friend, should you think you'll wait for a heavenly sign,
there'll be no angelic band, no anthems, no auld lang syne.
So reach out in faith, and in Jesus alone put your trust,
then stick everything on Heaven, for the Devil's hand is bust.

The Poet

I thought I might explode, lest I was able to write,
just one more poet, whose scribbling may never see light.
Is it just to release me from a bizarre past,
to exorcise ghosts and memories, or an autobiographical task.

I thought I might explode, lest I was able to create,
just one more poet, to ripple England's poetic lake.
But it's been said that the pen's mightier than the sword,
this I embrace, and dedicate my words to the Lord.

Love In The Shires

*(Remembering the 25th anniversary holiday,
Derby revisited summer 2003)*

Driving all day, driving till very late,
together at last, we drove the road of fate.
Cambridgeshire, Leicestershire, at Derby we rest,
a room for the night, a hunger to best.

Quiet Derbyshire lanes, Matlock Bath our host,
stopping for breakfast of coffee and toast.
No more miss you nights, lovers at last,
we're in Lancashire now, where lies only the past.

The Matrose

*(Written about St Mary's Church, Colchester,
which runs adjacent to the Roman wall)*

To tell of one Royalist Gunner, a King's Matrose,
who from St Mary's tower engaged his King's foes.
Climbing the church steps, cannon on his back,
he gained the necessary height to prevent an attack.

For days his skills kept the Roundheads at bay,
until inevitably the tower was shot away.
Known as Jack, but in rhyme this tale you know well,
for it's of his fall, and of Humpty Dumpty I tell.

Funeral Of An Innocent

(Written with Desney in mind - the last poem 1983)

Between outstretched arms,
a man carries his son,
that tiny white coffin,
held only by one.

Follows the Minister,
to a tiny graveside,
for baby Timothy,
too soon that final tide.

The poet might write,
blanketed by the good earth,
to a grieving mum,
lost for life, under cold dirt.

The Power Within

Many years now Lord, I've travelled Your road,
through highway and byway faith's carried life's load.
Your Spirit has taught me of the power within,
the armour of God, the faith in our strength to win.

To stand against a whirlwind of opinion and lies,
to fight and conquer whatever ambush darkness tries.
To stand for Christian values, a moral and disciplined call,
to fight and triumph over those who seek our fall.

A Father's Prayer

(Written for Ryan Keith Leese)

Sleep little son, sleep on while I stop to watch and pray,
The Lord I'll seek, to keep you safe and guide your way.
To keep you safe, in this disobedient and godless land,
Dear God I ask, hold him closely in the palm of Your hand.
To guide your days, that you might walk in the Father's love,
My Lord I ask, show him Your glory, Your kingdom above.

Sleep little man, sleep on while I stay to watch and pray,
The Lord I'll seek, to equip me as you grow day-by-day.
To love you, support you, and lead you until you're a man,
Dear God I ask, give me the wisdom to be more than I am.
To laugh with you, weep with you, to teach and to defend,
Lord, for my son here sleeping, help me to be his best friend.

Church Of Albion

My Lord, I know You to be monarch of every land,
yet it's in my native country that I worship Your hand.
Not for reasons of nationalism, not even for race,
but for love of soil, rich and blessed by Your grace.

I worship You in the beauty of an English sky,
in a newly ploughed field, in a solitary gull's cry.
I worship You in the strength of sea and shore,
this island scarred, healing from battle and war.

I worship You in the majesty of forest and tree,
to acknowledge Thy hand, is to walk with Thee.
I worship You in the loveliness of this our nation,
and thank God for this England, a gift of creation.

The Door

Courage knocked at the door,
a fugitive answered to its call,
to find no one there.

Happiness knocked at the door,
a stranger answered to its call,
to find no one there.

Romance knocked at the door,
a victim answered to its call,
to find no one there.

Insight knocked at the door,
a fool answered to its call,
to find no one there.

Success knocked at the door,
a loser answered to its call,
to find no one there.

The Son of God knocked at the door,
faith answered to His call,
and found salvation there.

A Man Called Hike Steele

(For Ryan, a response to your song 'Real')

I ran into an old friend today, a man called Hike Steele,
he rummaged through my life, he understood how I feel.
He'd known my good times, he'd even known my blues,
he examined my background and told me I must choose.
Whether to obey my calling, or to keep a safe distance,
to be a disciple, to follow and try and make a difference.

I ran into an old friend today, a man called Hike Steele,
he came with a message, a renewed challenge to reveal.
What's done is done, it's time to seek a new beginning,
minding less for the losing, looking more to the winning.
He's left me to my thoughts now, the mind and the surreal,
I think we'll only meet again, when dreams are made real.

Andrew P Nobbs

An accomplished and experienced *Writer Performer*, who possesses versatile speaking skills with a confident and enthusiastic nature.

Has a true love and appreciation of performing 'live' at a wide variety of venues. Adaptable to any environment with a genuine keenness to expand and build on current knowledge and abilities. Possesses a flexibility to work in all areas of media and entertainment, including films.

Relevant experience:

> Published poet, writer and stage performer
> Writer, director and producer of stage shows
> Experienced in working with poets, musicians and actors
> Worked in TV, film and media (including speaking parts)

Books:

> 1996 *Chasing Rainbows*
> 1997 *Discover Your Spiritual Force*
> 1998 *Inspirations*
> 1999 *Poetry Diary 2000*
> 2004 *Images Of The Soul, The Rivers Of Time*
> 2004 Take A Stand poetry anthology

Currently awaiting publication of Novella - *The Devil Is In Man*

Now

I woke then sat still.
My eyes closed
Then opened.
A cascade of colours
Ventured in through the window.
A humming sound in
The distance,
Birds adding to the
chorus.
A dryness in my mouth
a joy in my heart.
I am here
but I am nowhere.
Time transcends being
Being transcends time.
I wander through the house
Into the garden.
Touching, feeling, hearing, tasting
everything around.
I'm at peace.
I'm alive, experiencing magic, experiencing wonder
My present is with me
I am totally in my present
Now.

Listen

Listen upon a whispered prayer
Listen as people stop and stare,
Listen as time slowly ticks by
Listen as people start to get high.
Listen and take time for a moment's peace
Listen and take time for those who have least.
Listen to the echoes in your ear
Listen when everything is clear,
Listen upon a watery grave
Listen to the soldier, oh so brave,
Listen when people start to speak
Listen as an old lady starts to weep
Listen when everything has no sound
Listen put your ear to the ground,
Listen as children play and sing
Listen when all things start to ring.
Listen as the world goes by
Listen as people start to lie,
Listen as a baby starts to cry
Listen and just listen.
Listen until it is time to be heard
Listen then say your spoken word.

Miracle

To see the rise of the sun
Gently caressing the horizon sea,
To breathe in with total awe
And experience this magnificent show,
To plunge wonderfully immersed
In the oneness of life,
To feel the magic of its power
And touch the essence of the light,
To see the beauty from afar
Then witness the miracle you are.

One Day I Spoke To God And Said

If I could climb the highest mountain
Swim across the ocean
Fly to the stars
Then rest on Mars
God, what would you say?

If I could dissolve hatred and fear
And cure disease and tears
Then make love so beautiful and clear
God, what would you say?

If I could magic wonder across the universe
And with every deed of bad
Disappeared with good
God, what would you say?

If I could open everyone's eyes to the
Brotherhood of humanity
Then see the unity of nations complete
If I could do all this, God
And not be misunderstood
God, what would you say?

God replied with all his magnitude of power
My child it's not a question of if
But when, and when that time arrives
Then I will pray to you and you will be me

Universal Karma

A fireball of pleasurable pain
Twisted inside touching knowing
Breaking realms of mental gain.
I lay face down
I turn I shout and then calm,
Wonderful calm and then solitude
I survey my world all around
My eyes half-closed
To life's diseased and hungered bound.
I slowly reach the sky
And collect clouds passing by,
Drenched into my dripped coffee
Hot and cold then hot again,
Does this cycle cater from all this rain
As the universal karma
Cries out its pain.
The treasure within myself
Is the song I shall sing
Touching distant lands
Bringing hope where bleak is found,
My voice is heard
But the universal karma comes around.

Shadows And Light

Shadows and light showed some time spent
Jealousy and greed were not heaven sent,
Don't look for signs in every token
It is carried with every word unspoken,
Watch the tide move through each second
Then see life's reflection slowly beckon.

Shallow footprints and shooting stars
Flash a smile like broken scars,
Powerful thoughts strike each victim's mind
Until they wished for a time of kind,
Priests look without a second glance
But such a man can take a chance.

Wind, rain, sun and snow
Keep life's revolution on the go,
Flying like a bird on a winter's high
Takes man towards the deep blue sky,
Strike a pose, like a god on a stall
Looking down on the Earth so small.

Collect a thimble full of heavenly power
And throw it on Earth like a shower,
Pray for war, hunger and disease
To be finally rid and to cease,
Heaven and Earth to become just one
Then you will see my kingdom come.

Loan

I live inside myself looking out
I sometimes touch the emotion
From a constant distant shout,
I live and touch every experience anew
Remembering the lessons of forgotten blue.
As time passes across my brow
I remember the places and timeless faces
I may never see again.
Amused by open happiness along the way
As my eyes touch my possessions lost
I dilute the reasons for all my cost,
It is love that filled my heart to the brim
And took away all my broken forgotten sin,
People, places time and your wonderful home
I'm afraid my friend they're all on constant loan.

A Cup Of Coffee

Café
A cup of coffee
My pen, waiting for inspiration
Noise of laughter
Sun piercing through,
People coming, people going
The theatre of life.
Like actors waiting for their cue
Conversations caressing my ears
Not really knowing what's been said.
People's lives entwined
As caffeine dilutes their mind,
A piece of unbroken time.
Another cup of coffee
A kiss from a passing friend
'Take care, I'll see you later'
was his reply
a smile as she waved goodbye.
the star of the show
has walked on stage
admiring glances all around
a take-away sandwich, and a drink
It's enough to make everybody take a glance.
She passes dialogue with ease and style
And leaves with panache and grace,
I sip and pause
Then sip again
Waiting for my coffee's end.
An itch in my pen as I start to write
It flows with the beauty of life's light
I know now this moment wasn't to waste
As my inspiration came with my coffee's taste.

C'est La Vie

That's life
I said
When all
Was said
It had
To be
Was plain
To see
It's been
And gone
And was
Not long
Who cares
Not me
As time
Has gone
And time
Has come
Who cares

Not me
But then
And now
It's got
To be
The way
To see
For love
And now
There is
To be
A way
And how
But who
Could know
Who cares
Not me
My strife
That's life.

C'est la vie

Enlightenment

I've walked across soft silk sandy beaches
Pebbled shores and rocky mountains
Where water flows from time made glorious fountains,
Seen the red heat of summer suns burning
Generating energy to all who's yearning,
I've touched happiness and pain wherever I go
Tormented by the confused human flow.

Fighting wars created deep from within
Peace I craved never to win,
Finely stripped I nervously shared
My spirit was left wanting
And needed to be found.

Searching longing only creating emptiness
I finally found a place where I could rest,
As fish swim through darkened hallows
My heart wandered on through the sea
Blackened crushed and distorted from the core
Peace of mind I found from that unlocked door.

Gently pushing past debris scorn
I knew then my life had been worn,
Pockets of time completely blown away
Smoothly caressing those echoes from the past
Figments of imaginations joy taken from the last.

Fresh clear blue soul washes over toil
A moment's reflections keeps me forever loyal
Freedom from slavery's mental swollen hand
Hopes visions casts a message so long
Life's experience always cries there's no wrong

Suddenly sparkles of light appear to me
Destiny lurks as I capture the key,
Slowly turning as my thoughts race on
My journey's end was still a horizon beyond.
Enlightenment was mine never to be gone.

Converge Upon A Manic Day

Tracking down the memories from a weekend haze
Pushing your way past commuters' strife,
Like ants on a cerebral robotic mission
The feeling I get with all these people,
Their minds lost to earn their daily bread.

It's the mortgage, the ex-wife and the car
I hear one of them say,

But still they converge upon a manic day.
The train pulls up like a waiting tomb
To cure their ills and pills that kills and kills
And kills

Like sheep rotting to the core
They come to see the darkness light,
And again they converge upon a manic day
Waiting to earn their forgotten money.

Stupid carnations of spiritual boredom,
Living life without giving
Dying without ever living.

Masquerade

The mask of my painted discourse
Created illusion of past repression
Invented picture, empty vision,
Chosen cover of past submission.
Identity grained against the soul
Wanted to be what's not my own.
Expressing personality telling a lie
Radiating words from past life's shield.
Illuminating colours to many, and fool
Interpreting a shade of life's broken gold
My joie de vivre will never be sold.
Guiding my shadows fire to always give
To please that of being and what is,
To satisfy my illustrated desire
Covering the mirror and my chosen face.
I am what I must surely be
Take away my masquerade for all to see,
Fresh is the welcome from my imprisoned solitude.
The tears fall down without a trace
The world can see time was my wanton waste.

David Bray

I have always loved poetry - Blake and Byron especially; but talking of me, I started to write poetry some time ago, inspired and motivated by the Lord God. But my poetry is varied and my other inspiration is The Ladies Sweet Kisses.

But less of me, I'll leave you to continue with my poetry.

I stand in the shadow of greatness and I try to find that completeness within my poetry.

A Humble Self Portrait In Poetry

From the
Lowest class
In school
But I am
Nobody's
Fool but
A servant
Of the Lord
The one true
God who
Motivates
And inspires my
Poetry from
Paradise
I testify
I testify
That in the
Wink
Of an eye
The Lord God
Breathed on
The Earth
And gave
Adam birth

Spitfire

Spitfire
Spitfire
Soaring in the
Blue
Spitfire
Spitfire
The foe
To pursue
Spitfire
Spitfire
England
Owes to
You victory

Concorde

A product of British
And French minds
Beneath its delta
Wings the miles
Unwind that
Graceful nose
That bends in
Praise as she flies
The sky's highways
Soon in the blue
She will be seen
No more
And she has flown
Five million miles
Forsooth in the
Skies the Earth's
Roof.

The Cross On The Hill Golgotha

(To be read downward and across)

```
                    T
                    h
                    e
                    L
                    o
          The  r skull
   A serene d shaped stanza
      Praise G the Lord
                    o
                    d
                    D
                    i
                    e
                    d
                    S
                    a
                    c
                    r
                    i
                    f
                    i
                    c
                    e
                    d
                    O
                    n
                    T
                    h
                    e
                    u
                    k  l
                    s  l
      In Life is Death
```

The Rose

The rose lies
Resplendent 'neath
Heaven's azure
Crown
And the sun
So radiant
Painted gold

Nature's
Verdant
Glow

The breeze
Whispers
A natural
Melody

With fluted
Lips divine

And amidst
All this
Splendour
I taste
Life's
Sweet wine
And know
That
Thou art
Mine

The Tiger

Thy dark and fiery
Countenance
That roams the
Jungle's verdant
Heart
With fang
Mantled jaws
Armed with
Ferocity
With death
As companion
And killing
Thy art

To My True Love

She moves in splendour
As the day
And beams of light
Shall guide her
Way
Her breath is like
A whispered sigh
Her silken hair
And oh her
Eyes
Never to be
Dimmed by tears
The love we
Share with
No parting
Fears
She walks
Gracefully
Through
The years

The Font

This christened
Babe
The Lord will
Save so pure
That young
Soul
With a new
Name a
Christian
Flame
Submerged
In hydra
To save
The soul
That
Now
Answers
To the
Lord's
Control

Lady Diana

Her sun-kissed
Hair and face
So fair
Her bright blue
Eyes now from
Portraits
Glance
A royal
Bride
And Mother
Too
Our tears
For her
Now dry
So
Goodbye
Fair lady
Goodbye

The Universe

A work of God's love
And as I sit and wonder
At the universe
That we are under
Where the stars
Glance down from the
Astral skies with
Their bright prismatic
Eyes dwelling in
Their varied schools
Made of atoms and
Molecules and black
Holes vestibules and the
Planets' designated orbs
The sun and moon obey the
Master's plan and the
Astronaut within his
Speeding torb fills with
Thrall and awe his fellow
Man
Where the cosmos gleams
And glows and the meteors
And the meteorites with
Their fiery tails
That they with
The comets share
In inner and outer
Space
And the satellites
With their sonic
Voices and radar
Eyes communicate
With those below
And when all the
Lord God's work
Was done he rested

On the Sabbath
And he was pleased
With his works
And life began
And man looked
Up with hand
Shielded eyes
At paradise

Night Spotlight

In its velvet softness
The night draws its
Satin curtains and the moon
Glances down from its
Bed of stars arrayed
In light. The dreamer
Dreams the lovers sigh
The fox and owl hunt
Like angular shadows
Their dark trade
Is prophesied and made
Of stealth the bat
Hunts insects on the
Wing in its sonic flight
Trees reach for the
Vaulted skies
Flowers sleep their
Gossamer petals
Folded in rest
And above all this
Paradise blesses
All life

In The Dark Satanic Evening - A Warning

In the dark satanic
Evening of the dark
Satanic day

In the dark
Satanic coven
Where the witch
And warlock
Stray casting

Spells and voodoo
Curses on their
Unsuspecting prey
In the dark
Satanic
Evening
Of the dark
Satanic day